## Praise for *Bitter Freedom*

"A mother tells her daughter of the day by day horrors she endured during the Holocaust and how the thought of her daughter's safety kept her alive through incredible privation and suffering. For the daughter, it must be a comforting explanation of what happened and why she was seemingly abandoned. I found the book engrossing and hard to put down. It is an unassuming, genuine and heartbreaking daily record of the terror, genocide, privation, courage and heroism of the Holocaust. The afterword by the daughter Rena Bernstein, and a parallel account by another surviving family member bolster this unforgettable story."

Eileen Haavik McIntire
Author, *Shadow of the Rock*

"It is hard to imagine a more moving story written by a loving mother to her daughter. Revealed in a personal account of courage and devotion, the Holocaust takes on even greater meaning. It is truly the greatest human tragedy, but its horror inspired the greatest human goodness."

Brad Fisher
Senior Editor, Camino Books

# BITTER FREEDOM
*Memoir of a Holocaust Survivor*

**Date: 8/28/15**

**BIO WALLACH**
**Wallach, Jafa.**
**Bitter freedom : memoir of a**
**Holocaust survivor /**

Jafa Wallach

Gihon River Press
East Stroudsburg PA 18301

2012

Printed in the United States of America


Cover Design by Barbara Werden


First Gihon River Press Edition


ISBN: 978-0-9819906-3-7


Library of Congress Cataloging-in-Publication Data Pending

# DEDICATION

This memoir, *Bitter Freedom*, is dedicated, in memoriam, to my Mother, Jafa Wallach...the most courageous, kindest and most loving person I have ever known.

She saved us all...with her faith, her strength and optimism...and her indomitable courage...a courage I witnessed throughout her life.

Died: August 19th, 2011. Age 101.

Jafa Wallach

# ACKNOWLEDGMENTS

I want to thank all those who read my mother's manuscript over the years and encouraged us to publish it, especially Paul Rubens who organized the material and corrected the mistakes in English.

Above all, I wish to extend my gratitude to Alan Magill of *The Jewish Press* who has written extensively about my mother and her book while it was still in manuscript form.

I'm grateful to all the people at Tova Press and Hermitage Publications for making the 2006 limited edition of *Bitter Freedom* so beautiful and elegant.

My thanks also go to Steve Feuer and Gihon River Press for believing in my mother's story, and now giving it the national attention and accessibility that it truly deserves.

Rena Bernstein

My mother wrote *Bitter Freedom* in English so that my brother Sheldon (born in America) and I could know her story. She had been in the United States only a short time and her English needed some repair. Several decades later I corrected her spelling and punctuation...but left her words and her voice as she had written them.

—Rena Bernstein

**House of Representatives**

**HARRISBURG**
PO Box 202189
164A East Wing
Harrisburg, PA 17120-2189
Phone: (717) 260-6171
Fax: (717) 787-9185

Commonwealth of Pennsylvania
Harrisburg

**DISTRICT**

Physical:
RR5 Box 5221 B (Route 209)
East Stroudsburg, PA 18301

**COMMITTEES**
Human Services
Children and Youth
Tourism and Recreational Development
Commerce

**ROSEMARY M. BROWN**, MEMBER
189TH LEGISLATIVE DISTRICT

Mailing:
PO Box 869
Marshalls Creek, PA 18335
Phone: (570) 420-8301
Fax: (570) 420-8304

November 2, 2011

A mother's love is unconditional and forever engrained in our hearts. Often this love and devotion holds the bonds of a family together regardless of a tragedy that may occur. *Bitter Freedom* by Jafa Wallach shows the strength of that love and the will to survive. One mother conveys her 22 months of daily activities to survive and hide herself and family from the Germans.

As a mother, I could feel the love between Jafa and her daughter, Rena, and how she and her husband fought to protect their family during this tragedy. Not only did they fight to survive, but they realized that documenting each and every day would educate and help their daughter and others understand these horrific events if they were to survive.

The history of our own families is an integral part of who we are as individuals. Their family history became a time that reflects the real people who made our world what it is today. Their personal, family histories, characterize the day-to-day life of the Holocaust. Nearly 75 years have passed since the first Jews were persecuted for their heritage and religion. Today in the course of the 21st century, it is nearly incomprehensible to believe that such atrocities occurred. How could one man brainwash so many people to kill others? And how could no one know for so many years?

*Bitter Freedom* is a survivor's story. I applaud the courage and strength it took to communicate this story. My personal wish to the readers of this book is to remind them of the peace, equality and respect we must always show to one another. May we all remember our individual uniqueness and value each and every life.

Kind regards,

*Rosemary M. Brown*

Rosemary M. Brown
State Representative - 189th Legislative District
Pennsylvania House of Representatives

# FOREWORD

More than sixty years ago a nightmare ended for millions in the rubble, burned-out cities and ruined landscapes of war-ravaged Europe. For millions of others, however, it had already come to a brutal and vicious end in the ghettos and death camps of the Nazi regime. Only a few survived and for these, the ones who endured those fires of hatred and death, the nightmare can never entirely end. How do you live with the memories? How do you forget the loved ones left behind, the ones who couldn't be saved in the darkest hours of that blackest of all savage nights?

In September 1939, Adolf Hitler, the Nazi dictator of Germany, reneging on a pledge of peace he had given in exchange for acquisition of the Sudetenland, then a part of Czechoslovakia, brutally and treacherously attacked Poland, his neighbor to the east. He did this in tandem with the Soviet Union, a nation that had formerly been his enemy. Entering into a secret pact with Soviet dictator Josef Stalin, Hitler broke his word to the British and French over the Sudetenland compromise and took the western part of Poland for the German Reich while ceding the east to Stalin's Red Army.

Unprepared for this double onslaught, Polish resistance collapsed within weeks and the country, divided by the two invading armies, ceased to exist. The British and French, allies of the Poles, having previously dithered in hopes of peace with the mercurial Nazi dictator, were caught entirely unprepared. After watching Hitler rearm Germany in the 1930s, thus breaking the peace terms that had ended World War I in 1918, after standing by as Hitler further violated the terms of the 1925 Locarno Treaty by reoccupying the Rhineland, after watching him annex nearby Austria, and after having granted him a large part of Czechoslovakia in exchange for the promise of "peace in our time," Britain and the world were now witness to the brutal rape of a nation. Left with no honorable alternative, Britain and France finally declared war. But they were too late to prevent the dismemberment of Poland. The Germans struck swiftly, sweeping through most of Europe, driving British troops out of France and back across the English Channel at Dunkirk. A beaten and prostrate France collapsed before the Nazi juggernaut and Britain found herself alone on the other side of the narrow Channel.

Ever impatient of results and perhaps intoxicated with his own initial successes, Hitler halted at the Channel and did not attempt the crossing. Instead, after a period of consolidation in Western Europe, he stunned the world again and broke his previous pact with Stalin, turning on his Russian ally in June of 1941. Paralyzed and surprised by Nazi perfidy, the Red Army in Poland and elsewhere collapsed as the Germans swept into the very heartland of the Soviet empire itself. The world had not seen such audacious double-dealing in centuries. Backed by the German war machine, the Nazis won victory after victory in their rush to the east. And in eastern Poland, where the Soviets had only recently dismantled the old Polish institutions and structures, a new and more ruthless order now arrived as the Nazis dug in and began to use the people and resources of that conquered land to fuel their ongoing war against the Russians. For the Jews of Poland it was a disaster.

The Nazis carried Hitler's obsessive desire to rid the world of Jews with them into the east. What had been a difficult regime for Poland's Jews under the Soviet conquerors quickly grew into a nightmare of historic proportions as the Nazis systematically rounded up Jewish Poles and pressed them, first into narrow ghettos and then into concentration camps designed to work them to death or kill them outright. Where the Soviets had engaged in forced population transfers for resettlement purposes during their brief rule in eastern Poland—shipping many Polish Jews to the Siberian wilderness—the Germans soon proved they had something much more insidious in mind. The Jews in the conquered lands of Europe were taken by surprise, never dreaming that civilized men could do to their fellow men what was now being done to them. But so swiftly had the Germans come east and so comprehensive was their control of the lands they seized that there was literally nowhere left to run. Escape was made especially difficult by the willing accomplices the Nazis found in the local populations of the lands they conquered, lands where anti-Semitism was deeply and historically ingrained. But it wasn't ingrained everywhere...or in everyone.

*Bitter Freedom* is the story of a few Polish Jews who survived the Nazi terror despite being swallowed by Hitler's death machine, survived it because they were not alone. While many of their neighbors and fellow countrymen collaborated outright with the Nazis or pretended ignorance, a few stood apart, willing to risk all. *Bitter Freedom* is about these people, too, especially about one man who put his own life and family at risk for five fellow human beings, concealing four of them under the very noses of the Gestapo, even as he desperately schemed to preserve the life of the fifth, a four-year-old child.

Jafa Wallach and her husband, Dr. Natan Wallach, arrived in the United States in 1947, two years after the end of the great conflagration that convulsed mid-twentieth century Europe, and settled in Arverne in the county of Queens in New York City, barely distinguishable from hundreds of others in that small, lower middle-class community. An educated woman, Wallach and her spouse had lived through the worst the Nazis had to offer in Poland, witness to the brutal abuse, deportations and savage murders of that era. One fateful morning, by blind luck, the Wallachs escaped the slaughter visited on the others in a camp they had been consigned to and decided, then and there, to escape from the Nazis. With the help of a local man they had known for years, a Polish mechanic named Jozef Zwonarz, she and her husband found their way to the grim safety of his dank cellar and remained there for twenty-two months as Zwonarz scurried about aboveground, scavenging food and water to keep them alive and playing a dangerous cat and mouse game with the authorities to save the couple's four-year-old daughter from the death camps.

The Wallachs and a few other family members lived through the war because of Zwonarz's heroic efforts, while most of European Jewry did not. It follows that their story, and the stories of others like them, are important to us for they alone remain to tell what others now cannot. Each story like this is unique, reflecting the luck and circumstances which enabled the survivors to live to tell it. But because so many died, we're moved to ask how it was that these few didn't? The answers are in the very stories themselves, with their depths of pain and odd turns of circumstance, stories in which we may discover how tenuous the thread of life really is. A momentary meeting here, something glimpsed at a distance there, a decision to walk in one direction instead of another, an unforeseen lapse in a guard's attention...on all such things do our lives depend. And so it is with the events these people recall. Most of us don't realize the true fragility of our existence most of the time. But these people lived it. And it is with them still.

This book was written by Jafa Wallach over fifty years ago to ensure that her own story would not be lost. She wrote it for her daughter, Rena Bernstein, that same little girl Jozef Zwonarz and a few of his compatriots saved in the darkest days of the Nazi Holocaust. And the writing reflects that. It's written in straightforward prose, the voice of a mother speaking to her daughter, telling her the things she must never forget, the things that must be passed on to others. Grown now to maturity in her own right, Rena Bernstein has chosen this moment to offer her mother's tale to the world. It's a story for us all.

A simple tale, it recalls the dreadfully real disaster that overtook Jafa Wallach's large and close-knit family, the Manasters of Orelec, a small village near Lesko in Poland in the year 1939. Although Bernstein was herself only a small child at the time, she was present when the Germans and Russians arrived to destroy the only world she had known. Years later, in 1959, Jafa Wallach, her mother, wrote everything down so that her children would know what she had known. But the story never saw the light of day. There were so many stories of the Holocaust then. And no one wanted to hear...

Determined to bring her mother's account to the world, Rena Bernstein worked for years on the manuscript, shaping and polishing it, fact-checking and even returning to Poland, where it all happened, to see the house and cellar in which her parents hid for herself. And to find and speak with those who still remembered.

An artist in her own right, Bernstein now spends her days working in oils and pastels, remembering the images of a childhood passed in a strange and wild place. She remains deeply affected by the dimly-held recollections she still retains, memories of a child too young to grasp the gravity of her circumstances but old enough, even then, to miss the warmth of loving parents. She too has a story, a tale of being torn unceremoniously from the arms of her mother, only to be spirited into the woods by unknown people. It recalls the life she led in a forest hideaway, a life without the warmth of caring parents, a wild child in dark woodlands, unspeaking and rarely spoken to. Bernstein's recollections are partial and highly impressionistic, which is precisely what we would expect from a child's mind. But they offer a haunting counterpoint to the simple and unadorned prose of Jafa Wallach in *Bitter Freedom*.

Bernstein has put her story together for this book, too, and it appears in the Afterword at the book's end. Supplementing the tale further is a shorter piece, composed by Jafa Wallach's late sister, Helena Manaster Ramer, herself a survivor of the Nazi atrocities. Her experiences were quite different, though in some ways more harrowing, than Wallach's own. Taken together, these tales by three Holocaust survivors offer a spine chilling firsthand account of the worst excesses of which human beings are capable.

In today's world, faced with those who would deny the Nazi atrocities, and with those who would revisit them, it's more important than ever for the voices of people like Jafa Wallach to be heard. With over sixty years between us now and the end of that awful era, those who saw the worst mankind had to give with their own eyes are gradually leaving us. Soon there will be none to bear personal witness to the most monumental evil mankind has yet perpetrated on its own. What can they leave behind of greater worth than this, their own firsthand recollections of what has been a warning to us all?

Stuart W. Mirsky
Belle Harbor, New York
February 8, 2006

*For*
*Anna*
*Sheldon*
*Rena*
*Jonathan*
*Joe*
*and Brianna*

## In Memory of Our Immediate Family
### who perished in the Holocaust

*Joseph Manaster*
*Sarah Manaster*
*Abraham Joshua (Muniu) Manaster*
*Reisel Manaster and son Leibish*
*Lipman Klüghaupt*
*Esther Manaster Klüghaupt*
*with son Szulo and daughter Sonia*
*Abraham (Oskar) Schneider*
*Bronka Manaster Schneider*
*Mania Manaster*
*Samuel and Leah Wallach*
*David and Mina Wallach and son Alek*
*Natan and Sala Wallach and son*
*Hania Wallach*

## In Memory of

*Dr. Natan Wallach*
*Rachel Manaster*
*Jozef Zwonarz*
*Janek Konkol*
*Dr. Norbert Ramer*
*Helena (Hela) Manaster Ramer*
*Milek Manaster*
*Roman Elsner*
*Dr. Samuel Kessler*
*Clarisse Manaster Kessler*
*Pinek Manasterski*

# TABLE OF CONTENTS

# PROLOGUE

 number like six million doesn't penetrate the mind. It's too big to grasp all at once. The idea of the destruction of so many is beyond our ordinary understanding. But the story of one family, how some could not escape disaster while others survived, contains a message that can be felt and understood...and passed on, from generation to generation.

This book was written not long after World War II ended, when the memory of what had occurred was still fresh in my mind. For many years the manuscript sat in a closet. My family did not read it, and I didn't look at it again. We weren't ready to face our memories or to relive the pain of those dreadful days. And neither were others willing to listen to our experiences. When some of us tried to tell this story to other Jews we would be met only by incomprehension and sadness. Many would just ask us to stop, saying our story was too painful to hear.

Now it's time to bring my manuscript out of that closet. Across the planet, Holocaust memorials and museums have familiarized the world with what happened in those days to so many millions. This book, perhaps, can add something to that and illuminate what it felt like to be a Jew in those years, in occupied Poland. I do not speak now merely to show how much my own family endured. We were only some among many. Our story, though it's about my own flesh and blood that lived and died with us sixty years earlier, is also my children's story. It is for them that I first wrote these words in the years immediately after those awful events that began in 1939. I wrote this so they will know what I know, remember the people I remember, and never forget what befell us.

They must never allow it to happen to anyone again. Not to our own people and not to others. I want my children and their children, and all the children who come after us, to be strong in the knowledge of what has been so they may learn to rely on their own strength to defend themselves against evil, whenever and wherever it arises.

We have seen how people can be blind and deaf to the pain of others. To rely on such as these in the face of all the evidence of those years, to simply hope such people will change their ways, is a great mistake. Each of us must witness the horror for ourselves and take responsibility for our own lives and for the lives of those we love.

In the end, what remains is the belief that life, no matter how hard, is good. This alone is what we held onto during those dreadful years when we cowered in the darkness, afraid for our lives. And we believe it still.

We were glad to have survived and to be living now in a flourishing community once more, despite the efforts of those who hated us to extinguish the flame of our people. Whatever else can be taken from this story, this belief in the goodness of life is its heart. I hope it will speak to you and move you to hope, and to have faith in the future as I do.

Jafa Wallach
January 30, 2006

# CHAPTER ONE

# 1939

The years have gone by and yet the memory of how it all began remains vivid, fearfully close, as though it all happened yesterday. We were at home, Apartment #3 Jagielonska Street in the town of Sanok in Poland, listening to radio bulletins of Hitler's attack. You, my daughter, were just one year old. You looked up at our anxious faces, your father's and mine, but you could not have understood how deeply frightened we were. You repeated after us, in your baby lisp, "war, war"—the ugliest word in human speech. It wasn't long after that that German planes began to pay their deadly visits to our little town. Soon we would sit through several night raids in the local air raid shelter.

The German advance was rapid. As the Sanok Hospital staff and the Red Cross prepared to evacuate and move behind Polish army lines, the Polish government encouraged everyone, especially young people, to go east to form a front against the Germans. We were among the first contingents to leave town. I packed a few things quickly. Your father, a doctor by then, took only a few instruments in his medical bag. With you in my arms we left our home, leaving everything behind. We would never see it again.

By the time we had traveled 15 kilometers and reached the village of Orelec, near Lesko, word reached us that we must not travel farther. My father, your grandfather, Josef Manaster, lived in Orelec and insisted that we remain with him there, for there was danger on the roads. The whole region was being bombed. "You and your child will end up in a ditch by the side of the road," my father said to me. We decided to heed his advice. In the remote village of Orelec we should be safe for a while, we thought. And so we stayed.

My father's farm looked more beautiful than ever before my eyes, although there was the smell of war in the air and times were uncertain. My father, who had experienced the First World War and had foreseen the ruinous consequences of inflation, had invested all his money in the farm. He had put up new buildings and repaired the old ones and had selected the finest breeds of horses and cattle to raise there.

The year had yielded unusually fine crops. I remember your Uncle Milek bringing home a beet from the field that was almost as large as you were. Our barns were full of wheat and hay, the orchard heavy with fruit and the pond teeming with fish.

Our whole family had collected at the farm by the time we'd arrived, including your father's parents, Leah and Samuel Wallach, and his sister Hania. In these early days of the war, life on the farm seemed relatively peaceful. Certainly there was plenty of food, but the news was bad and continued to worsen. Each day brought word of the cruelties the Germans visited on captured Jewish soldiers of the Polish army. The news came to us from soldiers back from the front and by civilians fleeing the Germans and looking for some remote place of safety. Dozens of them stopped at our farm every day and we were kept busy cooking soup in huge pots, along with mountains of potatoes and barley to feed the hungry. Bread, normally baked once a week, was now baked every two days.

The Polish army was in retreat toward the East and army officers, their units destroyed, had fled and were hiding in the forest. They sent messengers to the farm asking us for help. Your uncles Pinek and Milek, my younger brothers, brought them food and civilian clothing and helped many reach the Hungarian border.

All of that was endurable. But the reports of what was being done to captured Jews were frightening. We heard about a group of Jewish soldiers buried alive near Ustrzyki, a small town in the neighborhood of our farm, and we shivered at the cruelty of it.

Geography was to play a crucial part in our lives. By chance, when the first dust had settled and the Germans and Russians had divided Poland between them, Sanok and Lesko became border towns facing each other across the River San. One marked the line of the German occupation zone of Poland, the other began the Russian-occupied territory to the East. I had been born in Lesko, your father in Sanok, at the foot of the Carpathian Mountains. With the German invasion and the division of Poland between the Germans and Russians that followed in 1939, the River San became a dividing line that would mean life or death for Jews.

The Jewish population from the West fled from the German occupiers to the East, to the Russian side. At first only men came but later families came, too, leaving behind all their possessions and homes. Hundreds of people crossed the San daily through Sanok and Lesko.

Because there was no transportation of any kind out of Lesko, everyone remained in this border town. But Lesko, a small town with a population of no more than five to six thousand was not prepared for so many people. It could neither lodge nor feed them.

But people kept coming. A fear beyond description seized them and drove them from their homes. Though initially driven by those fears, they were physically driven as well, later on, by the Germans who forced them from their homes. Sanok, across the river, was also crowded with fleeing people. Everybody ran from the Germans to the hope of safety on the Russian side.

Soon a Russian army unit arrived in Lesko and placed a border guard on the bridge. The Germans put their own guard on the Sanok side. But this did not stop the people from crossing the river. Men and women with small children in their arms swam and waded across the cold water. In the night they hid from the firing machine guns, but the guns and the river nevertheless claimed many.

Finally, after some weeks, the exodus stopped. An iron lock had been put around the two towns and the border was sealed.

It was in this atmosphere that we began to prepare for the High Holy Days— a solemn time made even more so by our circumstances. As usual, the services were held in my parents' house. Only our cantor, with his beautiful voice, was missing. Muniu, my oldest brother, who was living in Rzeszow, now under German occupation, was absent.

Though these holidays required strict religious observance, services were often interrupted to listen to the Yiddish radio bulletins from Minsk that promised Jews relief from German oppression. Songs of promise and hope were played again and again. We were glad we were on the Russian side of the river.

Before the war the border between Poland and Russia had been hermetically sealed. In fact, one could be sent to the Bereza Kartuska, the only concentration camp in Poland, for belonging to a Communist organization. We knew nothing of Communism in practice.

Now the Russians came into our town with songs and music. Russian soldiers mingled with the townspeople. Friendly and jolly, they passed out small change and candy to the children; there was dancing and music in the streets. We were all relieved when the Russians settled in. But as soon as the Russians began to feel at home, the Soviet takeover of Lesko and its surrounding area began in earnest.

Visitors came to our farm, two officers, looking, they said, for "ammunition." They took our jewelry instead. Then others came, looking for Pinek and Milek, who had been denounced for helping the fleeing Polish army officers. My brothers, who had hidden from the Germans, now hid from the Russians as well.

Finally the "community organizers" came. We were told that no one was to move from the farm and that we were to attend an important, general meeting in the village to hear important news. At the meeting the whole village participated and a Russian officer informed the population that our farm, on which many had formerly worked, would now be divided among them. You can well imagine the excitement this caused. Human beings are always glad to get something for nothing. My father was astonished at this turn of events and could only nod in silence.

After the meeting in the village, Russians came to our house. Our entire family was called together. The Russians turned to my father and reminded him that he was no longer the owner of his farm. It belonged to the people, they said, and we were not to touch or sell anything from either the house or the farm. "The property which you stole from the people has now been returned to them," a Russian officer pronounced grandly. "Furthermore, none of you is to leave this house until further notice."

When we protested, we were told that father was considered an enemy of the government and the people. As such, he and his family were to be carefully guarded. Several soldiers were left with us for the next few days. They took over the house and farm entirely and we had to cook for them and feed them.

One of them tried to be understanding. "Actually," he said, "you are a big family. Each of you should get a few acres of land and a cow so you could work and live." He flattered your father in particular, saying, "We like doctors. We need them and treat them well." But these friendly chats were often mixed with threats.

In the village the excitement was terrific. The Russians began to hand out "gifts" from the farm. First the servants and the poorest villagers received "gifts." One received one of our cows, another, a horse. Some got pieces of furniture. It was touching to see that many of the poorest of the local people were reluctant to take anything. The wife of the forest watchman even brought back the cow she had received. With tears in her eyes she told us she didn't want it. It took your uncles a long time to persuade her to keep it. It wasn't ours anymore.

The wealthiest peasants showed themselves to be very greedy and without consideration. They took whatever they could lay their hands on, as one grabs things from a fire: the crops from the barns and the fields, wood from the forest, vegetables, anything. None of them ever remembered such a harvest before. They glared at us and spoke to us shamelessly. We could not believe these were the same people with whom we had lived on friendly terms for so many years.

After several days we were permitted to leave — empty handed. The Soviet officials announced this to us while we crowded around them — as if awaiting a verdict. There were tears in my father's eyes. He looked broken. "What are we going to do?" he spoke aloud. One guard, who seemed moved by the scene, walked over to me and asked in a whisper, "Why can't you put on a few extra things?"

It was a good idea and we decided to act on this advice. Each of us put on a few layers of clothing, one on top of the other, and we walked out quickly, not even looking back at what had been our home.

We walked to the next village, Uherce, four kilometers away, and went to our friend's house. There we took off the extra clothing that was to prove so useful later on, when early winter came.

My father was the most heartbroken of all of us by the loss of the farm. Mania, next to the youngest of my nine sisters and brothers, was also very shaken by these events. Mania had loved the farm and had always helped my brothers run it. She did not give up now. She scurried from one official to another in an attempt to retrieve at least a small part of the provisions, clothing and personal items we had left behind in our home. She had some success: she received written permission allowing us to remove a few sacks of potatoes, some other vegetables and some wood.

And so we had a little food. But we still had the problem of finding a place to live. My father and stepmother secured a room in the home of Dr. Fink, one of their best friends in nearby Lesko. Your father's family found a little place in town, too. The rest of us took over a little empty house on top of a hill overlooking the railroad station in the town of Uherce. There we tried to recover from the shock and to slowly understand what had happened to us.

In town, the Russian occupiers moved into the administrative offices and began to install a new system of working and living. In all the neighboring farms the picture was more or less the same as it was with ours. After the Russians had finished with the landowners, like my father, the so-called "nationalization" spread to towns and cities. The industrialists, big and middle income businessmen, all were slowly divested of their possessions. Only small shopkeepers were temporarily left alone. Lesko, because it was a border town, received a more thorough cleanup for "security reasons" than some other places. Among the nationalized businesses were Manaster's, Guttwirt's, Teich's, Isser's, Freilich's and Fuchs'.

I remember an incident which occurred in connection with that nationalization. The daughter of Mr. Guttwirt became insane and ran down to Huzele, a border village where entrance was forbidden. People who saw her went to the guard, one by one, to intervene on her behalf. The amazed guard looked at them asking, "How is it that so many people are concerned about the safety of one insane woman here when with us thousands of healthy ones disappear unnoticed?"

Lesko was crowded with people. Since the war began, the population had doubled with newcomers. The large surrounding farms no longer delivered food and milk to town, so it was left to the small, private farmers to feed the population, and they took advantage of the situation. Prices began rising daily. Very soon there was a shortage of everything. No one could remember this ever having happened in Poland before. This way of life—standing in line for hours waiting for bread and milk, and everything else—was something new and very unpleasant, especially in a year of plenty like that one.

Within a few months hunger appeared. The winter came early that year bringing frost and heavy snows. The newcomers, who had fled their homes in summer clothing and without money, were cold and hungry. Sickness spread throughout the town. Your father and Dr. Lisikiewicz hurried from house to house, helpless to do anything since there were no drugs or medicines of any kind readily available. Yet a few weeks later they managed to set up a clinic and infirmary.

Then my father, your grandfather, was ordered to appear at NKVD headquarters. He was questioned for hours, threatened with jail and worse, and finally released. This happened twice. Somebody let him know that he had better leave town.

The younger members of my family had already left for Lwow to find work and a place to live and reorganize their lives.

Finding a job was not easy. Everybody had to register for work and give his or her autobiography: where one came from, what social class, what kind of occupation one's parents had. My family had a great deal to cover up. One was naturally luckier to have had a shoemaker or a tailor for a father than a *pomeshchik*—a landowner.

My family took over a bombed apartment, fixed it up and finally found work. Each of the children got a job and they even found one for your grandfather when they brought him, incognito, to Lwow. It seemed as if, for them, life would normalize again.

My sister Bronka married and moved into an apartment with her husband Oskar. Your Aunt Hela became engaged to the man who would be your Uncle Norbert.

We remained in Lesko with your father's family, although in separate quarters. Our home was two rooms in the attic of a Mr. Birnbaum's house, so cold your hands froze. But this was all we could find at first. Next to us, in one room, was a family from Krosno. Eight people in one room. They, too, were cold and miserable—and, like all the others, were waiting and hoping for an opportunity to return to their homes.

Shortly, such an opportunity came, or at least it seemed so at the time. The Russians began a registration of the population in town. They announced to the newcomers that those who wanted to return home would be permitted to and those who wished to remain would be accepted as Russian citizens and receive a passport. A majority of the newcomers registered for the return... not because their prospects at the hands of the Germans seemed any better than their present existence but because they yearned to reunite with their families.

We registered to stay. We had no reason to go back. There was little to go back to. Only my oldest brother Muniu and your father's older brother, David, and their families were on the German side. The rest of our families were in Russian-occupied Poland. The only other members of the family, your Aunt Clarisse and Uncle Sam, had left home in 1937 for Italy where Sam was a medical student.

Things were lively in town during the time of registration. The Party needed to be kept informed about what everybody said and did, and a lot of young people were put to work to procure information. They proved to be extremely diligent and hardworking informers.

Then, after we had gone through the procedural questioning, we were given special identity papers. But they did not authorize us to venture within 100 kilometers of the borders of Russian-occupied Poland. This, of course, meant we were going to have to move again.

By pure chance, your aunt Esther, my eldest sister, and her husband, Lipman, were given papers which would have allowed them to stay. Then a clerk recognized them and they were called back and had to take identity papers which required them to move. Esther and Lipman left Lesko shortly afterwards with their two children, beautiful and talented 11-year-old Sonia and her sweet six-year-old brother Szulo. They went to live with Lipman's family in Sambor. We never saw them again. Lipman belonged to the Yolles rabbinical family, whose children and their families numbered more than one hundred. They all perished.

It took us much longer to decide where to go and to leave town. Daddy had to belong to the medical society of a town before he could go there to practice, and that town had to be far from the border. It seemed that everywhere we turned there was a border, so it was not easy to get a position. We decided to go to Lwow first, to see how the rest of the family was and to ask their advice on what we should do.

Passover was approaching as we prepared to leave, and the Jews of Lesko, busily baking matzohs, were more cheerful. They looked forward to this family holiday. We, too, hoped to be with the rest of the family in Lwow. But then, suddenly, you and I got sick, both of us with high fevers and infections of the middle ear. Daddy went to the mayor of the town to ask permission for us to remain longer due to our sickness. But permission was not granted and we were ordered to leave immediately.

The journey to Lwow was hard. You cried with pain the whole length of the trip and I myself was very uncomfortable. But our stay in Lwow didn't last very long. The place was too small for the whole family. In addition, Daddy's parents were now also with us. As such, we were constantly in each other's way. Most important of all, your father had to look for a position without delay. It could not be put off.

We had barely recovered, you and I, when he left to go through Russian-occupied Poland. He visited various medical centers looking for a position but returned disappointed. He finally decided to go again to the same county medical facility in Drohobycz to which he had belonged while in Lesko. To his pleasant surprise, he was approved and assigned to be a physician in a town near Stryj called Lisiatycze.

Lisiatycze, we found, consisted mainly of Ukrainians with some Poles and a few Jewish families, all of them farmers. We were soon on friendly terms with them all. They were especially fond of your father, who was of course their physician.

The farmers were very dissatisfied with the new way of life the Russians had brought with them. They often complained about it. They couldn't accept the idea that a government official would tell them when to sow, when to cut their wheat, when to harvest it. They had always used their own judgment about these things. The result was that in one area the crop was still green when it was cut, and in another the heavy rains severely damaged the standing ripe grain before permission could be obtained to cut and harvest it. It was hard to believe that this kind of thing was normal Russian procedure on the soil of the Soviet Union itself, but in Russian-occupied Poland these and similar practices were prevalent.

Law and order soon began to reign. Schools were opened and there were clinics, hospitals, and maternity wards in practically every village. A physician at such locations was quite a busy man. Everyone without exception had to be vaccinated. The physician was required to give informative lectures to the public on the value of preventative medicine, including vaccinations and periodic check-ups. Those who were sick were cared for and given medication free of charge.

Every month your father had to provide a written report on his activities to the Party. There was a lot of other paperwork for him to do as well. In the beginning he worked alone but later a Russian nurse was sent to help him. In some instances she was helpful, but she also helped keep us under surveillance.

At the beginning, when we arrived in the village, we had become friendly with some of the other professional people and had managed to get together with them socially a number of times. We did not know that such meetings were frowned upon. Now we were warned against continuing them. We had to be careful. We were not registered in the town as required. We were not 100 kilometers from the border. We were quite close to the border, in fact, and there were air bases around our house. For some reason, negligence perhaps, no one had asked us to register when we had arrived; later they never asked about it.

After the warnings to stay away from social gatherings, we lived an isolated life. Physically, our circumstances were good. We occupied a nice little country house, part of it used for the medical office. Father received instruments and supplies and a monthly payment for his services. There were additional payments to cover fuel and electricity. What we needed most was peace and tranquility.

Your father continued to organize medical services in the area. In this he was aided by the mayor of the town, who helped persuade the local people to get inoculated against various diseases as was required by the authorities. The peasants were reluctant to take the shots because these were followed by a day or more of high temperature. They had to be informed of the necessity for taking the injections.

Very soon people began to take advantage of the free medical service. They began to come for unnecessary examinations. Now, many times during the night, your father would be pulled out of bed to attend to someone. Any slight discomfort which one was too busy to attend to during the day became a good reason to wake the doctor at night.

There was plenty of trouble with the officials, too. No matter how hard your father tried to follow the various regulations, there were so many of them, and they were so confusing and contradictory, that it was easy to go astray. The first two months, for example, your father's monthly reports displeased the local officials. For such a large population he had too few patients. "Only a counterrevolutionary could work that way," he was told.

Your father began to work even harder. Practically everyone was vaccinated. He treated more colds, deliveries, infections, etc. The figures in the next report were much bigger. But he was reproached again. "How is it," asked his superior, "that after months of treating people there is now more sickness than before?" Nevertheless, he added, he should not worry but continue his work.

Life in Russian-occupied Poland continued. Election day came and the population was informed that everybody was required to vote. At dawn commissars appeared at the homes of senior citizens, taking them to the polling places. The following day newspapers printed the names and pictures of these senior citizens, stating that they had been so eager to vote that they had stayed up all night in order to be first at the polls. Later, comparing voting percentages of the capitalist countries and the USSR, these papers pointed out that Soviet citizens are happier and healthier than their counterparts everywhere else and vote more readily because of that.

Another indication of this was the induction process into military service. Your father had to examine all men fit for service. According to his professional opinion some men were exempted from service as not physically fit. This made the commissar assigned to the induction board very unhappy. He ordered your father to reexamine those he had exempted. Everybody was fit for some job in the army, the commissar explained carefully. The newspapers were making comparisons at that time between the health of citizens in the United States and the U.S.S.R. In the United States, the newspapers claimed, the draft rejected 40 percent but under the Soviets only two percent were rejected.

As time went on we grew accustomed to the place and the people. You were running around happily and loved to help with the gardening, especially with picking green peas and stuffing the pods into the pockets of your apron. We watched with pride as you grew and developed, hoping wistfully for the war to end soon.

My father, unfortunately, could not stay long in Lwow with the children. After two or three months, he had to change places again because somebody had denounced him. After searching for another hiding place he finally wound up in a small town called Rosdol, near Stryj, where he lived incognito.

Life was uncertain for everybody. From the German side of Poland came bad letters from Jews. In Sanok, in the first days of the German arrival, the synagogue was burned and when a Jew tried to save the holy scrolls he was thrown into the fire and burned to death. Letters reported things like "uncle *brod* (bread), uncle *zuker* (sugar) very seldom come to see us." It was especially hard for the women who were left behind with small children, their men having earlier joined the Polish army and later having remained with the Russians.

Although things were hard, even in these hopeless circumstances divided families longed to reunite with their loved ones. When Russian officials began to announce the coming of a citizen exchange with the German side of occupied Poland, people became excited.

That day finally arrived. It was, if I'm not mistaken, during the spring of 1940. Big signs were placed everywhere—on telephone and telegraph poles and on the walls of buildings throughout occupied Poland. The signs announced the final registration for people wanting to go back to the German side. Those desiring to do so were told to pack and prepare.

For two days there was lively excitement everywhere. Clerks in the offices were very busy registering people. People stood on line for hours so they wouldn't lose their chance to register and return home.

In Lwow, that day, Bronka's employer confided to her that things were not as they seemed and that matters would come to a head the following night. Handing her the keys to the office building, he said, "We don't want to know who you bring in here."

That evening she did not come home from work. She moved like a shadow among the buildings, from street to street, collecting people.

And the streets were not as quiet as they usually were at that time of night. Hundreds of different kinds of vehicles moved back and forth. Armed soldiers and NKVD patrols paced the streets. Others were engaged in forcibly entering houses wherever registered people lay sleeping, dreaming of happy reunions with their families.

Then the sleepers were awakened with alarming knocks at the door. Pulled out of their beds and forced to dress quickly, they hardly had time to take anything with them. Only then did it dawn on them that it was not home they were being taken to.

For two days and nights the hunt for registered refugees continued. Those found were loaded into freight cars meant for animals. Carefully guarded, the trains stood in the stations for two days awaiting orders to move.

In the meantime, the cellars, attics and closets of Bronka's office building overflowed with people. Only after the transport left did they feel secure enough to venture out into the street. It was a morning after a long nightmare. Everyone felt dazed, not knowing what to do or what the next day would bring.

The following day we received a call from Bronka. She described what had happened and warned us to stay close to home and to talk to no one. We hardly needed the warning. Who by this time did not know that silence was necessary for survival?

Then, eight or nine weeks later, we received a letter from Novosibirsk. It was from a friend of ours, Ida Rosenberg, from the old days in Sanok. It was the first communication we had from the people who had been taken away in cattle cars. They had been taken deep into the remote forests of Siberia. Ida described the torment of the long journey and the place where she and almost the entire colony of refugees from Sanok had been brought. We wondered how such a letter had reached us, and were afraid of the possible consequences.

We read this letter many times and shed many tears over it. We needed to send food and medicine right away. I made egg barley and dried it (there was none readily available as we have here). We sent food in concentrated form so that it should not take up space and weight—and would not spoil as quickly. The first parcels also contained all kinds of emergency medications that we could obtain for heart disease, for bleeding and insect bites, sulfur drugs for infections, aspirins, alcohol, cotton, gauze, soap and many other things.

We began to receive similarly heartbreaking letters from other friends and relatives. The letters told of people dropped into virgin forests in the vastness of Siberia. Some had to chop down trees and build their own places to live. Others were housed in old log barracks built by previous deportees. The food and medical care were of the lowest grade. They told of food that could be eaten only because the alternative was starvation. And the food went only to those who worked. Everyone, the very old and very young and those who were sick, had to work...or starve. There was no protection from the severe frost and snow, nor, later, from the hot sun and the plague of various insects. Sanitary facilities were almost nonexistent. The result was inevitable: illness of every kind and epidemics that took thousands of lives.

In a letter, Ida wrote of once asking the man in charge if any of the deportees would ever be allowed to reemerge from that Siberian hell. His answer was "*nicagda*" (never). As it happened, he was wrong—at least for those who managed to survive. A large number of people actually did return when the war ended. But the suffering and death of the Siberian experience remains another grim chapter in the tragic history of Polish Jewry in World War II.

For us, living in a Polish village under Russian rule, it began to seem after a time that the chaos accompanying vast shuffling of people was at last beginning to moderate and that people were finding work and places to live. Hundreds of Russian families now settled in occupied Poland, renamed the West Ukraine. These new settlers took over the best apartments in the cities and towns. And they brought with them money. They were wonderful consumers. They bought everything they saw in large quantities, as if there was never going to be any more. The shopkeepers gazed at these people with astonished eyes even though they were delighted to do such good business. Their delight, however, was short-lived. Very soon they learned there were no replacements for the merchandise they sold.

But for the transplanted Russians, their new situation could not be more glorious. They found the apartments and offices where they now worked to be luxurious beyond anything they had known. They marveled at the beautiful clothing, furniture, etc. Everything was vastly better than in their homeland. When they were told the price of an object they simply did not believe it–they called it propaganda.

Watches were one of the most attractive items and greatly coveted, so much so that all kinds of jokes about this passion began to circulate. One expression, referring to the strangely corrupting power of watches, was: "With a watch you can shoot down a pilot." Occupied Poland was a paradise for these Russians. "One learns about good living from these capitalists," they said.

CHAPTER TWO

# THE HORROR BEGINS

June 22, 1941, was a Sunday. The day had been declared a special holiday to celebrate Russian achievement in aviation. The local populace had been invited to come to the nearby airbase for a day of festivities and we were invited to ride with you in one of the airplanes. You were very excited about it and couldn't wait until Sunday morning.

At dawn on that Sunday we were awakened by shooting from airplanes which were flying very low over our heads. We thought perhaps this was some trick flying, introducing the promised celebration. We hardly had time to dress when a thick cloud of smoke and sparks came in through the open windows and doors. The entire air base was on fire.

The Russians standing nearby were surprised, too. In the first few minutes they did not seem to realize what was going on. Soon no one was in doubt that this was no celebration but a German attack.

We had to leave at once. Your father went to hire a horse and wagon and in between the waves of attacks we packed. We left Lisiatycze and, toward evening, arrived in another village.

The Ukrainians there looked at us with devilish smiles. They were waiting for the Germans to return and make good their promises. With Ukrainian cooperation, the Germans quickly took the territory back.

We were disappointed to see the Russians preparing to evacuate with no attempt to bring in fresh forces to counter the German invasion. The Russians now set up their defense line farther east at what had formerly been the border separating the Ukraine from the rest of the Soviet Union. Before they left, the Russians gave the population a choice to remain or retreat with them. Many Jews went with them. They were afraid to meet the Germans again. No other citizens in Poland were really disturbed about who the boss would be. They only had to remain in their homes and their possessions were increased with each tragedy that struck their Jewish neighbors. Such opportunities were many.

We were in a dilemma about whether to stay or go. We had aged parents and a small child; it would be difficult to move with the Russians. But to remain with the Ukrainians and the Germans promised to be even harder. Within a few days, the decision was no longer ours. The Russians barely had time to leave when the Germans began to arrive.

As reward for their help, the Ukrainians received a few days in which they could do what they wished with the Jews. Jews were no longer protected by law.

A shiver goes through my body when speaking of those days. An organized group of young Ukrainians, under the leadership of a man named Sicz, let terror loose throughout the country. Their sadism and murderousness were equal to that of the Gestapo. They descended upon a village and, after a day spent in drunken revelry, murdered and plundered at night.

The local priests called for mercy in God's name, but theirs was a voice in the wilderness.

It was at that time that your father was called to attend an emergency: The daughter of a family named Sticura, whom we knew well, was in premature delivery. He was gone for hours and, by late afternoon, I began to be really worried and terrified at the prospect of being without him as night approached. I decided to risk going to the Sticuras' myself. Leaving your grandparents (your father's parents) and his sister Hania with our Jewish neighbor, a man named Jonas, I hurried through the fields with you running to keep up alongside me. Your father was still there; the daughter was still in labor.

Old Mrs. Sticura was friendly. She prepared supper for the entire family and asked us to join them. As her daughter's labor wore on, Mrs. Sticura invited us to stay the night. We gladly accepted the invitation and retired to our room right after supper. I put you to bed and sat with you while your father continued to care for his patient.

That night we did not sleep. There was a commotion in the village, secret meetings, lively discussions and then screams mixed with wild laughter. A roving band knocked on the door of the Sticuras' house several times, demanding the doctor's family come out. The Sticuras did not let them inside and, because they were important people in the village, the toughs went away. The awful sounds continued throughout the night.

Curiosity arose in the village because we were in the Sticuras' house for so long. The next night the same thing happened, only this time the knocking was more frequent and the demand that we be turned over to them more insistent. They argued with the Sticuras but, because they were so respected and because a member of the family needed medical help, they finally went away.

For three long days Ukrainian thugs massacred any Jews that came their way. Finally, having delivered the baby, the Sticuras told us our family was safe and that we could now go home. We soon discovered that besides us a few other Jews in the village had survived.

Plundering and robberies of Jewish houses everywhere now became daily occurrences. One night a wild knocking and shouting to open the door awakened us. Your little body was rigid with fear. A few Ukrainians with rifles on their shoulders ordered your father to take you from my arms and that I follow them.

They came to a house and we stopped. Inside, a number of people were sitting around a table, eating and drinking. Among them was a young woman who recognized me and who pleaded with my abductors to let me go. They seemed to ignore her request but when we walked away they returned to our house, ordered me to remain and wanted your father instead. It is impossible to describe or to remember how many times one's heart stops beating at such moments.

For close to two hours your father was conveyed around the town. Then he was given ten minutes to awaken the rest of the Jews in the village.

Forced into the street, they stood there in abject fear of the Ukrainians. Suddenly, several Czech soldiers assigned to patrol the bridges passed by. When they saw this gathering in the middle of the night they walked over to the group and asked what was going on. They didn't wait for an answer, however, but ordered the Ukrainians to release your father and the other abducted Jews. Then they arrested the Ukrainians. Your father was able to come home.

After this incident we left for Stryj, a town of about 40,000, because we were afraid to remain longer in the village. We rented a room in a gentile section on the outskirts of town and lived there for about two months.

While pogroms occurred in other places, Stryj remained relatively quiet. The military command that took over the town after the Russians left assured the Jewish community that, as long as they remained, there would be no violence. They kept their word.

But a few weeks later, when this army contingent left, the Gestapo took over and hell was unleashed.

A *Judenra*t, a council of Jews, was appointed by the Germans to act as an intermediary agency between them and the local Jewish population. Food was rationed and distributed through this committee, as were demands for laborers. Soon huge sums of money in the form of so-called "contributions" were also extorted from the Jewish community. Jewelry and all valuables were collected to pay this ransom. And every day new laws and regulations pertaining to Jews were enacted and had to be strictly obeyed upon penalty of death.

In the first week of the Gestapo's arrival, the first slaughter of 1,200 people, mostly businessmen, took place. I happened to be on the street when a truck filled with Jewish people, young and old, passed by. A young Ukrainian, not in military uniform, stood there in the truck mercilessly reigning blows upon the hapless prisoners. I stood and painfully watched the truck until it disappeared down the road.

Each day now was filled with fear, and the nights were worse. We were exhausted by the constant moving but terror drove us on. We heard that Lesko was peaceful and we decided to go back to our home town. The next morning, the first day of the High Holidays in 1941, we were in a one-horse carriage on our way home. Your grandparents were in the back seat. Papa, with his open prayer book, prayed all the way.

Our journey was a safe one. The weather was beautiful, one of those Indian summer days when nature is dressed in many colors. The skies were so blue and the embrace of the sun so pleasant. We passed village after village, glad not to be noticed by anyone. Peasants were working in the fields, taking in their harvest of vegetables and potatoes.

We arrived in a village about twelve kilometers from Lesko. Since it was already evening, we decided to stay the night. You were very tired. All along the way each time we stopped you asked if we had reached home yet. You were too young to understand the situation. Luckily, we found a Jewish family who agreed to lodge us for the night.

The next morning we arrived in Lesko. A few German *Schutzpolizei* were stationed there under the leadership of a Viennese whose nature was not so rough. We obtained two rooms in Freilich's house, where young Mr. Freilich and his wife and two children lived at that time. We became friendly neighbors and later, when Jews were imprisoned in their homes and were unable to go out after curfew, it was good to have somebody to talk to. Soon after we came there, one by one, my family returned to be together again in our home town. Only my older sister and her family remained in Sambor.

People looked on us with envy, that after all our trials we were so lucky to be all together again. Soon all the people forced by the Russians to leave Lesko slowly returned home. Everyone felt that it would be easier to live through the war among old friends and gentile neighbors one had always known.

Unfortunately, the town was not left in peace for long. As had happened everywhere else, the Gestapo eventually arrived. A *Judenrat* council was formed to fulfill every German demand. For a Jew to be alive, he had to be useful.

And so all of us had to register for work. We received one pound of bread and nothing else for a whole week. Work was unpaid. Every day contingents of Jews were delivered to the sites of roads, new building construction and demolition. They worked on new, wider town sidewalks on which they were, themselves, forbidden to walk. They worked in fields and forests; they dug canals—all of it unpaid.

A Jew was not permitted to buy or sell anything to a gentile. He could only walk on the outskirts of town. He could not venture outside the town limits without special permission, which was granted only to work gangs.

Jews were ordered to wear white armbands with the Star of David. When one forgot and went out of the house without it, he found death. Armbands became excuses for beatings and persecution. At one time you were told the armband was not in the right place, at another it was not clean enough or not pressed.

You couldn't be found in the street, not even during the day, unless you were going to work. In the very beginning, neighbors could still gather in a home for prayer services. Soon, however, this too was banned and other gatherings were also forbidden.

The gentile population could get Jewish labor, if they wanted it, for free, and most of them did. Many Jewish workers received no food and returned home after a whole day's work hungry and, of course, without pay. Jewish laborers went daily to the lumber yards, forests, neighboring estates, factories, etc. The hunger among the Jewish people grew greater each day. Money and jewelry or other valuables were a thing of the past as we were systematically divested of everything we had. Even so, a secret exchange of clothing, linen and other items for food, which a peasant secretly brought to Jewish houses, began. But soon this ended as well. There was nothing more to exchange.

Signs of hunger soon began to occur. Hundreds of people were daily knocking on doors, begging for a little soup, a bite of bread, a few potatoes. Everybody, even the elite of the town, went around begging for crumbs. There were more of those who were asking than those who could give. I will never forget the three-year old twin girls, their poor tiny bodies wrapped in pieces of a *talis* (a prayer shawl), whose picture appeared in the German Gazette for the amusement of the population. These two little girls came to our door daily, begging for a piece of bread.

One day I saw a friend returning from work, her mouth painted green. Before I could even ask, she explained that she had been working in a field where grass grew plentifully.

Before my eyes I can still see my friend Beckey, swollen like a puppet, his eyes barely visible in his bloated face, asking for a little boiled water to fill his stomach.

Jews could no longer know the news or be educated. Jewish children could not attend school, belong to a library, or buy books or newspapers.

In the meantime, nobody knew how the Germans were doing on the Russian front. Nevertheless, we were told that our furs were needed to protect the German soldiers from the cold Russian climate. Thus began the so-called "fur action." Every Jew throughout the land had to relinquish his furs or any garment with fur trim. If a piece of fur was found in a Jewish home after the collection, the family was shot. Some people tried sabotage. They clogged the toilets and canals with fur; they cut them in pieces and burned them if they were able to. Our friend, Jozef Zwonarz, whom everyone called Józio, had hidden some of our furs when the war began. But now he decided it was too dangerous to keep them any longer. In the middle of the night he went to Uherce, where friends of ours lived, and burned the furs in their oven. The smoke and smell of the burning furs carried a long way. They were all terrified but the operation was successful.

Our acquaintance with Józio dated back many years, when he came to work for my father. He was a very fine mechanic, able to repair all kinds of machinery and vehicles on the farm. A generator he had installed supplied light, not only to the farm but to the entire village. Sometimes he stayed with us for weeks while he was working. The whole family liked him. He had a reputation in the village for being a good-hearted and broad-minded man. And this may have contributed to his lack of means, for his patience and kindness were often taken advantage of. People delayed paying him and, although he was the only mechanic in town and was always loaded with work, he was very poor.

Shortly after the incident with the furs, an oxygen tank exploded in Józio's face when he was working in his workshop in Lesko. He was badly burned. Your father treated Józio, and he came to the house often because of that. It gave us a chance to talk as we ate the vegetables he brought from his garden. (Poles, of course, were still allowed to eat.) Every bit of news he had he shared with us. Later when things became increasingly more frightening for Jews, he seriously considered ways to help us.

Meanwhile the Gestapo carried on its sadistic, beastly work. Among the first murdered of the town was the Guttwirt family. One Friday afternoon a Gestapo man came to their door and ordered the entire family to go to the Zaslaw concentration camp which was then being organized. When they arrived, they were shot—the entire family. A child of 18 months was saved for last. Even the Gestapo man who murdered them later said he would never forget the child's face, with its eyes bulging from its sockets. A woman accused by her neighbor of stealing beet leaves from her garden was also shot. Later, two young boys, Werner and Fuchs, Sima the fish-handler, who was forced to put on a *talis* before his execution, and many others whose names I can't remember, were in a group of seventy people brought together to the Lesko cemetery. There they had to dig their own common grave. Then a few shots were fired into the group and they were buried, most still alive. Sima's last words were a plea that they would be the last Jews to die in the town.

The next day the Gestapo ordered the rabbi and your father, as the local doctor, to supply statements attesting that the murdered people had died of natural causes. They did this to prepare for future contingencies.

Life had become a torment, no peace day or night. The nights were even more terrifying than the days. Every night I slept with you in a different place: under the roof, in the cellar, wherever I felt it would, for the moment, be safer. You were frightened and would ask, "Please let me sleep in my bed, I'm so uncomfortable here." One began to fear the burden of continuing to live, but the fear of torture and death was even greater.

Jews from the provinces of Sanok and Lesko were now concentrated in Lesko. The reason given for this was that these

Jews were going to be given work assignments. Many were killed, instead, in the course of being rounded up. Those that survived to reach town could find nowhere to live. The shelter for displaced persons was the local bath house and some synagogues. I have no words to describe the tragedy of these people. They were living and sleeping on their bundles. No hygiene, no food, no clothing. The Jews of Lesko were starving and couldn't do much for these others though everyone tried.

Each day brought more hard work for the only Jewish doctor who was himself helpless. Your father was tired and broken, but he had to go on. Each time he was called out at night I stood motionless at the window, waiting to hear the sound of his footsteps.

The first death from hunger was a boy next door, age sixteen, who had always been healthy and handsome. Starvation is frightful. People's faces become swollen, their eyes sink and are without a spark of life. They become totally unrecognizable. Some died as they walked in the street.

CHAPTER THREE

# THE CONCENTRATION CAMP

My sister Hela was a nurse and her husband Norbert a doctor. Hela and Norbert decided one day that the safest place they could be was in our native village of Orelec. There, with only two Jewish families in the whole village, they hoped they'd be overlooked by the Germans. So, together with Norbert's mother, they moved in with the Shenesells, the family of our former milkman. For a while the strategy worked. Then came the morning when all the Jews in the villages in the area were surrounded in their houses, dragged out and brought to a field near Olszanica. From this group only three survived—one for only a short time. From the grave of 500 people that remained on the field of Olszanica, at nightfall of the same day, the wife of Max Sun crawled out. A peasant who watched her crawl away finished her off.

The two other survivors were Hela and Norbert; the Germans thought they might still have need of their professional skills.

That tragic night Hela and Norbert, in great distress, came to our house in Lesko. The next day the Gestapo was in our house looking for them. Luckily for all of us, they were away when the Gestapo came. Your father was able to get a statement from Dr.

Lisikiewicz, an Aryan doctor, that Hela was seriously ill and needed an immediate operation. With this statement they received permission from the local Polizei commander, who was Viennese, to leave town.

Zwangsarbeitslager Zaslaw was built near Zaslaw, a town between Lesko and Zagorz, as a labor camp. Soon all the Jews from the region were concentrated there. By 1943 they would all be dead.

While the Germans were busy liquidating Jewish communities, in ways even the devil couldn't think of, the Gestapo had great interest in keeping up Jewish morale, especially of the remaining work groups which were needed for the German war machine. After each mass liquidation some rumor would arise to convey the idea that this slaughter had been the last. And the ever hopeful Jews believed each piece of "good news" when it came. They believed in what they wanted to believe. A rumor spread that the Germans were in headlong retreat on the Eastern front and that the war would end in a few days. News came from the ghetto in Sanok, confirmed by the local Gestapo, that Hitler's pictures had disappeared from the walls of the railroad station. This meant either a revolution in Germany or the end of the war. Something of great importance was happening, but nobody knew what. The local Gestapo remained silent. Jews were permitted to go into the streets that afternoon to await one of the leaders of the Jewish community, a lawyer named Dr. Teich, who had gone to Sanok to check on the truth of the amazing news.

"It's true," said Dr. Teich, after returning from Sanok with tears in his eyes. There was a huge babble of joy from the crowds, cries of happiness, embraces; people kissed and hugged and exchanged the tender and solemn greetings of the High Holy Days.

And then, a few days later, came the *aussiedlung*, the transfer to Zaslaw, taking us all one step closer to death.

Similar tricks and "good news" appeared before and after each slaughter, and each time we told one another, "Have you heard? It's good again."

I now lived with but one thought in my mind: where and how to hide my child before we were forced into the camp, because children were in the greatest danger. Our Józio came up with an idea. He would take you to his niece whose husband was in the army and was now a prisoner of war. She had moved with her little girl to the town of Zagorz to be near her family.

We planned carefully. Józio's niece agreed to take you to be a cousin to her little girl. I dressed you but could not answer many of your questions. Józio came and took you to the suburbs and on the way he told you about the aunt you were going to live with for a while and about your little cousin with whom you were going to play. Earlier, your father and I had also tried to prepare you and told you we would come for you soon. You couldn't understand the danger you were in but somehow you must have sensed the importance of this decision and you went with him. With a heavy heart your father and I remained at the door when you left.

We stood there in the doorway a long time, watching until you were out of sight. Finally I shut the door and there was a dizziness inside my head which I knew came from the endless thinking and talking about how we were going to find a place to keep you safe. It was still there, the uncertainty. Was this the right way? We knew that Józio was a good man and could be trusted. He had promised us that he would come to see you every day and watch over you, and we believed him. But he was only one man, betrayal could come from anywhere. For all our scheming and planning, we had ended by setting you adrift in a frightful sea, and it didn't help to tell ourselves that we'd had no choice.

One long day went by, and then another. We missed you so much. We didn't eat or sleep. Time moved very slowly. All our thoughts were with you. Were you quieter now? Were you learning to accept your new family, the strange surroundings? Would we hear about you soon? We hadn't seen Józio since and we were expecting him with hope, waiting for good news.

Józio had stayed with you until nightfall and then he left, with a promise to visit you daily. On the third day he came to tell us that he was going to bring you back. The three days you stayed there you had not stopped crying, refusing to take any food or drink.

Józio's niece had inquisitive neighbors who began to ask questions of a religious nature, whether you attend church, which one, etc. No amount of explanation seemed to satisfy them. They immediately suspected you were a Jewish child. Józio's niece became frightened and demanded he take you back to us.

Your father and I went to the outskirts of the town to meet you. As a doctor and nurse we had a little more freedom of movement than other Jews. And then there you were. We were happy to have you back for a short while. But now every minute with you was precious because we knew we had very few left. In just ten days we were to be moved to the concentration camp at Zaslaw. But we didn't give up hope of finding a secure place for you.

The opportunity came sooner than we expected. Józio found a mechanic, a friend of his, whose brother lived in the forest. He thought you would be safe there, at least for a little while.

It was Friday, September 6, 1942. We were all given freedom to walk around the town. The doors of the morbidly silent houses opened and people poured into the streets. Everybody knew what was in store, but there was nothing one could do about it but pray. And that is what we did. The whole desperate, despairing congregation of Lesko, under the leadership of the town rabbi, resolved to summon God to a *din torah*, a trial. The chosen place for this frightful event was to be the old cemetery. There on the grave of a long-dead rabbi still revered by all of us, black candles were lit. All the Jews of Lesko attended as Rabbi Horowitz pronounced the questions:"What do You do to Your beloved people? Why are You permitting Your people to be destroyed?"

Everyone was overcome, crying out to God about our situation. Finally, amidst the graves of our ancestors in Lesko, Rabbi Horowitz delivered his verdict: the Jews were not guilty. We were being punished without cause.

Later, as he waited in prison on the eve of Yom Kippur with 300 others, knowing that all were about to be killed, he told people it was all God's will. No one, he said, should try to evade the will of God. What we were enduring was akin to the sacrifice of Isaac.

It was Sunday, September 8th, the day before the *aussiedlung*, the complete transfer to the camp. All day long we waited for Magda and Janek who were coming to get you. We had talked to them for a long time, begging them to keep you for at least a few days until we could learn what the Germans intended to do with us. When you saw me crying before Magda you said, "Mommy dear, don't cry, you will see, we will live." There is a proverb that prophecy comes from the mouth of a child.

Everything was arranged, but to our disappointment no one came for you. In the twilight of that unforgettable day, when we had given up hope that Magda would come, she finally appeared. As you were standing there, undressed, crying and hiding behind me, she took you forcefully into her arms and walked out of the house. Like stones we remained standing at the window looking after you and Magda, who walked straight out of town toward the forest of Bezmiechowa, where she and Janek lived. We learned later that she had gotten out of town safely. Helped by the commotion in the town, she was able to pass through with a crying child, unnoticed.

That day, too, something unusual happened in town. A neighbor of ours died of a heart attack. Nobody ever remembered a funeral so well attended. All the Jews were present to see off a happy man to his eternal peace. At the same time one had the feeling one was attending one's own funeral.

A shout in our ears brought us all back to gray reality. An SS man was standing in the crowd near our house bellowing short instructions. Each person was to go to his house and have all money and jewelry ready for surrender to the Gestapo. Then we were to pack quickly and, at the stroke of midnight, every living soul, with all his possessions, must wait in front of his house for the Gestapo to collect the keys.

Can you picture the town, with all its thousands of Jewish inhabitants sitting in the night in front of their houses, on their bundles? It is hard to describe the picture and the feeling. Nearby, children were crying on their mothers' knees, wailing aloud, "Mama, I want to live" ... as in normal times they had asked for candy. Children believe that everything is in their parents' power. A weeping mother answered her little ones that they should run and hide themselves in the cemetery.

Many parents tried to save their children by sending them to different places, which ever seemed safest at that moment, only to be horrified when their children became the first victims. Two families sent their little girls to their home town a few days before the transfer. The next day, when half the population was taken away, their children were right there with the rest. Ah, the bitterness for those parents!

You never knew what was best to do. No ingenious undertaking succeeded. Everything ... everything failed.

But one thing at least came of the incident of the two little girls: we learned the truth of our situation. The explanation the Germans gave for taking away all these people was "resettlement for work." Belzec, where the two little girls were taken, was supposed to be a work site. To find out what had happened to their little girls the parents sent a gentile woman from Lesko all the way to Belzec, following the transport. There she found a place of horror—an isolated place, fenced in with barbed wire, where chimneys of crematoriums and gas chambers were smoking day and night.

There was no longer any mystery, though the Germans continued to reassure us that they needed people for work.

The first victims were always the sick, the old and the children. I will never forget our ninety-year-old neighbor who, with a friend equally as old, had decided to hide in the building when the Germans ordered us out of our houses. They were determined that the Germans would never take them alive. But as soon as we were out in the street and a frightful silence fell over the buildings, the two men, scared to death, ran out quickly to be among their neighbors.

The Gestapo went from house to house, collecting keys and putting a seal on each door. The silence of the night was disrupted by shouts from the Gestapo and their Ukrainian servicemen pacing the streets with dogs that could tear a man to pieces. In contrast to this noise, one could hear the heartbreaking cries of children and the whispered sounds of prayer from the dry lips of exhausted human beings all around us.

The journey began at daybreak. Wagons packed with people and their bundles moved out of the town. From all directions, horses and wagons converged on the road to Zaslaw. We moved slowly, step by step.

Your father and I were among the last to leave Lesko. Our thoughts were constantly on you. We kept wondering what had happened to you. Had you quieted down or was Magda bringing you back? We were afraid Magda had been caught. There was not a thing we could do. We had entrusted you to people we had known for only a short while because Józio had recommended them. We hoped you would be lucky. We were all in God's hands now.

All day long the transport continued. Twenty-two thousand people were gathered together that day, September 9, 1942, in a few hundred meters of space containing six buildings. This was Zaslaw. A paper factory was to have been built on this site. In the yard there was one toilet and one water fountain, near which long lines of thirsty people collected.

Our possessions were piled high and set on fire. Thick smoke hung over the huddled people, darkening the sky. We were choking from smoke and dust. A picture came into my mind, a picture of the Jews gathered around Mount Sinai to receive God's word. Here again we were gathered, I thought. Only this time for a different purpose, for sacrifice.

When we arrived in Zaslaw and saw the horrifying chaos there we decided to run back to Lesko—many kilometers away. We wanted to be sure that Magda had not brought you back and left you there alone. We hoped that our absence would not be noticed in the confusion.

We slipped away and made our way back, arriving in Lesko late in the afternoon. The town looked dead. Not a soul was in the street. We walked around, through our house and many houses and backyards of our neighbors. We looked at all the blank windows and they seemed to look back at us. We listened carefully, intently, for any possible sound, but there was nothing. Not even a cat meowed. It looked as though everything had disappeared with the inhabitants.

We made our way back to Zaslaw again. It was all dimly lit chaos with people trying to find places to sit. Swollen legs could no longer carry the exhausted bodies. Your father often wondered afterwards, and still cannot find a medical explanation for it today, why, under such circumstances, nobody fainted, no heart attacks occurred, not even among the elderly cardiac patients. All lived to be packed into trains for Belzec.

The night there was an unforgettable horror. We tried to find our relatives and friends who had been brought to Zaslaw from the countryside. We found your Grand Aunt Itta, my father's oldest sister, sitting on a bundle of rolled up bedding. She was blind. I knelt down and greeted and hugged her. When my face was against hers, I could feel her tears. "But where is Mina?" I asked. Mina was her daughter.

"Isn't she here?" Aunt Itta said, surprised. Just at that moment, Mina came, eight months pregnant, her husband and other children behind her. Everyone asked about you and where you were. I told them I didn't know and it was true—I really didn't know. But one thing I did know: wherever you were would be better than being with us there.

In the midst of this horror most of the people still believed they were being resettled. One had to believe in such moments.

It was late in the night. Exhausted heads, eyes shut, were resting everywhere on the ground. I could see an old man not far away, reciting the psalms of David over candlelight. In another corner a mother was feeding a baby. At another place there were familiar faces, people of our own family. And so we waited. No one was eager to see the daylight. Nothing good was expected. Everyone hoped and prayed for a miracle to happen.

Suddenly, like an answer, we heard the sounds of bombing in the distance. The echo of it pierced our bodies. The Russians were bombing the train factories in Sanok. Then the planes retreated. In the morning two doctors and their wives committed suicide ... to avoid seeing Zaslaw in the daylight again, I imagined.

You know how Zaslaw looked on that first memorable Monday so you can imagine how much worse it looked and felt as Tuesday dawned when the people from the Sanok ghetto were brought in.

It was again just before the High Holidays, the third and saddest of the Holidays since the war had begun.

On the following day, Wednesday, trains arrived on the rails next to the camp and a process of "selection" began. The aged were separated from the young, men from women and children. The old, the women and the children were put to one side. Here was the judgment: A German decided who shall live and who shall die.

Families huddled together, determined to share the same destiny. Older people shoved younger ones forcefully into the line of those "capable of work." Total strangers added their voices to the clamor, telling those who still hesitated to leave their parents, their smaller brothers and sisters: "Go out from here! You haven't lived yet! You have time to die!"

For a moment one felt a resignation in the group, a feeling of "we are tired of this life we have lived for so many years." The hunger pangs in the shrunken stomachs were unbearable. The tired swollen faces seemed to be saying that there is nothing to fight for. But suddenly a spontaneous murmur broke out. When the Gestapo started to push the people into the trains, many began to fight. They kicked and bit the Gestapo; they spat in their faces and tore their uniforms. Some tried to provoke the murderers to shoot them on the spot rather than allow themselves to be pushed into the railroad cars. A number of people died this way, among them the heroic Chuler girl.

She was between eighteen and twenty and she tried to provoke an SS man into shooting her. She kicked and spat at him and tore buttons from his uniform. He grappled with her, trying to push her onto the train. He could see she wanted him to shoot her and he wouldn't do it. He was enjoying his sport.

She pulled others into joining her, into resisting being loaded onto the trains, and they rallied around her. Finally, seeing that things were getting out of hand he did what she wanted and shot her.

The rest of us, those who still remained, watched all this unfold in terrible fascination, as though rooted where we stood. Then the long train lurched and started moving. It gave a long, loud whistle that rang in my ears for a long time afterwards. To this day I cannot bear to hear a train whistle like that.

The whole frightful scene was repeated that Friday when a second large transport, packed with frightened, shivering people left the station.

For the small group of us that remained, a new life of torture began. We were all registered for work. Everyone had to find some place to be a worker. The Germans again began to insist that workers were needed and they assured us that there would be enough work till the end of the war.

And so they started to organize workshops. Several rolls of cotton and wool cloth were salvaged from the huge pile of burning possessions, and from these beautiful dresses, blouses and other items of clothing were made. The knitwear workshop provided sweaters. Everything we made was shipped to Germany. People worked and hope rose again in our hearts.

Men whose wives and children had been taken away on the transport walked around like ghosts. They rebuked and blamed themselves for not having joined them. You could hear some very pious people disputing and denouncing with bitterness everything they had ever believed in and hoped for. But among them were also some optimists. Among them I especially remember Abraham Bart of Zarszyn. Bart was a Zionist, a follower of Jabotinsky. He managed despite everything to find ways to keep us from falling into complete despair. He would often sneak out of the gate and disappear for several hours. In the evening he would return with food, books, newspapers and, most of all, encouraging news. One day he brought news about an underground legion making its way, across Europe, to Palestine, and of the possibility of joining them. But most of all, best of all, was the news he brought that the front was moving closer to us.

In spite of the circumstances, life in the camp went on. There were some weddings. Every moment of life was precious to us; we lived for them, not knowing what tomorrow would bring.

But people still fought over a morsel of bread, even while walking to their graves. I remember the young, intelligent Kalman Horowitz, Pinek's friend. He had only one wish: to once again know the feeling of a full stomach before he died.

The fleeting nature of life was only too real for us. Death came with incredible suddenness, to groups of people and individuals alike. Executions were common. The Gestapo commandant of the camp, who took some strange satisfaction in being addressed by the Anglicized name of "John," had a number of deadly habits. One of them was to conclude his eating and drinking parties with a shooting match. We, the prisoners, were the targets. Sometimes target practice would be more specialized: infants and small children were picked up by the hair and thrown up and shot in midair like birds.

After a two month reign, "John" was killed by his friend Miller. There was a rumor that he hadn't been brutal enough with the people in the camp.

By this time your father and I were no longer in the main camp but in Lukawice, part of a work party of 120 people sent to toil in a lumber mill there. We were now under the supervision of a civilian from Hamburg named Salzman. We lived in a group of small bungalows encircled by a fence which separated the camp from the rest of the village.

The fence wasn't needed. None of us would have escaped. There was no place to go and hide. The reward for finding a Jew was 300 zlotys, the value of a pound of butter.

Our group of 120 included a few women. We cooked, cleaned and washed for all. We had more to eat than they had at Zaslaw, mostly cabbage and potatoes. It was more peaceful where we were, too. The Gestapo was not around.

Our group began to grow with the addition of many who sneaked out of Zaslaw, especially older men and women who were in greater danger there. People who had escaped into the woods joined us too.

And so some two months passed. There had been no word about you—two months of not knowing whether you were safe or not. Then, one afternoon, I was called to the gate. Your father followed me and we couldn't believe our eyes. Janek stood there. We were incredulous. How had he known where we were? How had he made his way here? And he had done all this for us? He brought news of you and told us you had quieted down and become a little acquainted with the new family. You were fine, he whispered. Tears of happiness choked us. I couldn't say a word.

I only wanted to hug and kiss him but too many eyes were upon us and I stood very still. Oh, how afraid we were. We had to be sure no whisper of this reached the Gestapo. We gave Janek some clothes we had left and some money we had managed to keep hidden and begged him to keep you, to take care of you. Then we quickly turned away and left.

Our lives were transformed. Suddenly we had the strength to do anything, any work they gave us. We had the strength to plan our survival. We couldn't imagine that happiness simply did not radiate from our eyes, that it was not immediately apparent to anyone who looked at us. We were sure people were looking at us strangely. We argued about whether we were imagining it or not. I felt guilty and ashamed to be happier than the others with whom we lived.

We were still at the lumber mill of course. Your father's parents joined us there—the rest of the family remaining, though, in Zaslaw. Life at the mill under the German civilian, Saltzman, was relatively peaceful. Saltzman liked to talk. Once he had gotten to know us a little he would walk over to your father, permit him to take the lumber off his shoulders and rest for a while, and have a chat. Once he discussed with your father the outcome of the war. He said, "What good is it that almost all Europe is in our hands? We still won't have *lebensraum* (living space)." He then explained to your father that the German mind is ingenious and will solve the *lebensraum* problem. "After the Jews are liquidated," he said, "we will liquidate the Poles and Ukrainians. We will get our *lebensraum*."

Life passed by slowly but there was hardly ever a quiet day or night. News from Zaslaw was terribly depressing—each day more so. The sadism with which the poor victims were treated before they died is beyond description. One had to undress, go into the grave and wait there for the merciful shot to be fired. The shot often struck the wrong place, like a foot or a hand. More than one bullet would not be wasted on a Jew. The still living victims were often buried alive with the dead.

People fought with their tormentors and many would not obey orders. An old rabbi refused to give up his *tallis* (prayer shawl) in which he was wrapped. Fighting for it, he managed to tear off a piece and wrap it around his otherwise naked body. An older woman refused to undress completely, saying that even her husband had never seen her naked. She was forced to undress even so. Mr. Reich, from Zagusz, had to remove the clothes from his own children, but then was not allowed to die with them. The Germans pulled him out of the grave. They could not deprive him of his terrible wish, however. At the last minute he jumped back into the grave and was buried alive there.

One little girl, six years old, remained alive almost to the war's end. Alone, she cared for herself. During the day she would sneak out and beg for food in the village. At night she returned like a shadow and found somewhere to sleep, a different spot every night. You never knew when she might be near, listening intently to every whisper. Even after the entire camp had been liquidated she still survived, maintaining herself like a cat in the nearby village. She was finally caught by the Ukrainians and killed three weeks before liberation.

I remember the cantor of the synagogue in the town. I will never forget his beautiful voice. On the eve of Yom Kippur he was being held in the jail with the other men of Lesko, Rabbi Horowitz among them. All were about to be murdered and buried in a mass grave. Then this man, this cantor, began to pray and to chant the ancient *Kol Nidre* so beautifully that it even touched the heart of the murderers listening outside. The Gestapo sent for the cantor and freed him. But not for long. Soon he was swept up in yet another transport and slaughtered anyway.

Among us there was a young shoemaker named Moishe, a good shoemaker who made boots for all the German and Ukrainian officials. The boots and shoes were so well made that many Germans shipped them home to their Fatherland. But then, inevitably, they would want him to make children's and baby shoes, too, and that's when the trouble started. Even though he was tortured and threatened with death, Moishe would not make children's shoes. He was bitter about the loss of his own children. Our efforts to persuade him did not seem to make any difference. Finally he agreed to make one pair of children's shoes in exchange for whiskey. After drinking, he made baby shoes.

Moishe mourned the death of his family, perhaps more than anyone else. Each time he brought a finished pair of shoes to a gentile house, he returned sick. He would then lay on his cot and refuse to eat. When asked what had happened, Moishe answered that he had seen a happy home—a child playing on the floor, a mother cooking, the warm aroma of a home cooked meal, the peacefulness of home life. All of this had not existed for us for years. The scene from normal life he described seemed so strange to us, so wonderful, a cherished memory of the past, a pious wish for the future—someday, beyond the darkness.

We were luckier than Moishe. We still had you and the thought of you helped us whenever we remembered the horrid things we had lived through. It helped us to have courage to deal with whatever came our way each awful day.

Our Józio came to the gates quite often now. He always brought us hopeful news. Everyone knew him and, when he arrived, anxious faces leaned toward the gate, listening. How we all wished to see the end of that war. Survival had become a holy duty for all of us. The weaker the body, the stronger our spirits seemed to become. We must not break. We must hold on despite each trial. We had to live!

The good news of German disasters on the front always came with other news of the speedy liquidation of Jewish communities. The daily reports of hunts for Jews in forests and caves made our blood freeze.

Through all this we waited anxiously for Janek's next visit, hoping for good news about you, expecting a little picture of you which Janek had promised to bring as a palpable sign you were still alive. You and Janek and Magda and her little daughter Stasia all lived in the forest in a remote little watchman's cottage.

We did not know that the danger of your remaining there had increased. The Gestapo had come a number of times, checking identity papers. They had questioned Janek. Frightened, he decided to send you to Lwow to stay with his fiance for a few months. And so, once again, you were living in a strange house, with a strange family, this time as Janek's niece.

At last Janek came to see us again. He brought a little photograph of you in Lwow. He promised to bring you back to his cottage after the hunts were over and to care for you regardless of what might happen to us. It was the last time we saw Janek until the liberation.

I kissed your picture, making it wet with my tears. Like a talisman, I carried it next to my heart at all times. You were our inspiration and hope to survive.

We looked forward anxiously to the long promised Allied invasion and second front. People were trying to stay alive in every possible way. We heard from some sources that Aryan papers were being produced. These identity papers provided one with a gentile name and background but for a very high fee. Many of these documents proved to be inadequate frauds, worthless, though once you had them it was too late, the money you paid for them was gone. Even so, some single persons managed to escape from the camp and live as gentiles. Living that way was difficult. You had to mix with the population, find work and a place to live, and avoid being recognized and denounced. Denunciations were a daily occurrence.

The constant dread and fear that such a life produced are indescribable. A new kind of cottage industry in the complexities of discovering and concealing Jewishness flourished. The gentile population had become "expert" in Jewish physiognomy, language, pronunciation, movement, gestures, etc. New occupations were born of this. Some gentiles lectured on the subject while others went into the business of remaking Polish Jews so they looked and behaved in every way as gentiles. Some were sincere in their intentions while others wanted to exploit Jews, to take everything they had left.

You remember, dear, our friend Ela, who survived disguised as an "Aryan"? She was engaged as an English tutor in the family of a high ranking Polish official. The family approved wholeheartedly of the destruction of Polish Jewry and often expressed this to Ela. She told us afterwards about horrible nightmares this caused her, describing how, at times, screaming in the night, she would be awakened by her hostess. She had to give the family an explanation so she told them devilish apparitions afflicted her sleep. They believed her. The thought never occurred to them that their beloved "Marya" was a Jewess.

There is a fascinating sequel to this story. A high ranking Polish official, a friend of the family, fell madly in love with Ela and tried to persuade her to marry him. He wouldn't listen to her careful attempts to turn his suit aside, not even when she alluded to a "certain something in my past" of which she was sure he would not approve. Nothing, absolutely nothing she could tell him about herself would make him love her less, he swore, or weaken his desire to marry her. Years later, after the liberation, she wrote him a letter and told him she was a Jewess. He answered: "I would like to see you just one more time—I would like to understand how I ever could have thought that I loved you ...."

In the first days of December, 1942, we were brought back from Lukawice to Zaslaw. We were sorry to leave Lukawice but could do nothing about it. All others who had been sent to different places were returned to one concentration point: Zaslaw. A few hundred boys who had worked at the Kirchoff Road construction project in Trepczy were also brought back, and locked up without food. The next day they were surrounded by the Gestapo with machine guns. A short fight began. The young boys fought with their hands. Of course the fight did not last long. Only one of the S.S. men was wounded.

CHAPTER FOUR

# ESCAPE

I was shocked at the sight of my poor father when we got back to Zaslaw. Clearly, conditions at the camp were frightful. All that could be said was that the whole family in the camp were still alive. Outside, however, death had already struck the family. Before we left Lukawice we had managed to send someone to Sambor, to my older sister. We learned that Lipman, her husband, was dead and that my sister Esther and her two children were faced with what would soon be the same end as the ghetto there was liquidated.

We had the awful feeling that these were the last days of our lives as well.

We had planned with Józio to make a hideout but nothing was as yet prepared. There was good news from the front and in their desperation people ran into the woods in the wild hope they would soon be liberated. But most of us knew better; we sensed that time was running out for us. A new proverb was coined: "Five minutes to liberation; four minutes to death."

December 1942 marked the beginning of an early and hard winter. People froze to death in the forest after a few days of hunger and cold. This made the others come back to camp of their own free will. The Germans no longer even bothered to guard the gates.

My brother Pinek overheard a comment made by the head of the camp, just as he left for Germany on a Christmas furlough: "The Poles will guard these Jews even better than we could."

The Gestapo even left the camp unguarded for a few days as they celebrated the holidays in Sanok. For some, this was a sign to remain in camp. For others, it was a sign to escape and for those freezing in the forest to return.

December 16, 1942 was a day of wild shooting. The Gestapo swooped into a workshop where 400 women sewed clothing, knitted sweaters, finished the seams on gloves and prepared other such things to be sent to Germany. They began to play cat and mouse with the women, chasing them from corner to corner. The women ran out, the guards shooting from behind.

Your father and I had awakened early and were walking through the empty courtyard on our way to get breakfast. Suddenly a guard appeared, grabbed me by the arm and shouted, "Take this one too!" He pulled me toward the workshop of screaming women. I ran blindly and fell into a stack of hay used to feed the S.S. horses. The hay covered me. In the confusion I wasn't noticed.

After a long time the shooting stopped. Spread out over the yard were young girls in the first bloom of their lives, now dead, lying strewn about like fresh-cut wheat. Then the murderers went to breakfast while the cleanup was in progress. Another mass grave was prepared on the outskirts of Zaslaw and the bodies were thrown in. The mound of earth moved for a long time afterwards as the hot blood of the victims lifted the mantle of rubble and dirt. After the liberation we were told that before the Russian front neared our region, all graves were opened and the contents burned.

On December 17, the day after the massacre of the girls, I convinced your father that we had to escape, no matter what the danger. The panic and torture of our life in the camp had become unbearable. In our desperation we sought to find a hiding place and then bring out the rest of the family. Even so, we had no illusions about our chances. Whatever we did, danger and death were everywhere.

A group of workers left the camp that morning and the three of us, your father, uncle Pinek and I, were among them. We had a work permit. It was a cold and nasty day. As we neared Lesko, our group of six went in different directions. We all agreed to meet again at nightfall.

Lesko looked like a ghost town. The empty houses with their broken windows and open doors seemed to speak of the tragedy of their inhabitants. The streets and the big square in the center of the town had not yet been cleaned up and were littered with books, papers, and pictures. Pieces of holy parchment, bibles, and *talesim* all lay strewn in the mud. Everything precious and holy was in the dust. Darkness, hate and destruction had triumphed.

We wandered among the silent houses which three months before had been filled with people. Every so often we'd stop and pick up a discarded photograph. Our minds were preoccupied with you. Then it began to rain hard and your father remembered a patient he had been treating before we left Lesko. We decided to go to her home until darkness fell.

The gentile family was happy to see us because their little girl was sick with a high fever. While your father was examining the child, our hostess spoke to me. She asked about my child and my eyes filled with tears. My response seemed to move her and I saw tears in her eyes, too. The woman expressed regret that we had to return to Zaslaw.

As soon as it became dark we prepared to leave. At the last moment, our hostess brought out a large, home-baked loaf of bread. We thanked her and then went out into the dark street.

Luckily it was still raining and we were able to sneak into Józio's house unnoticed. He had been waiting for us. He opened the door and, after we entered, he left, locking the door from the outside. Pinek returned to camp, planning to rejoin us in a few days.

The room we walked into was dark, the windows covered with blankets. Things were scattered around; wire, tools and broken glass on the beds. We were alone in the house.

The house we found ourselves in was a very little, very old country house where Józio had lived with his wife and four children. His oldest daughter was then fourteen. His workshop had been there too. But the house had to be repaired and so Józio had moved his family to another house, just in time to give us shelter. The workshop continued to operate, however.

As I said before, Józio was a fine mechanic, but he hardly ever made a comfortable living. He had a philosophical approach to life and the things that were important to most people seemed to be secondary to him. He was understanding and helpful and never seemed envious of others. All these virtues, because they yielded no income, became faults in his wife's eyes. She complained constantly about all the things they were missing. He tried hard and was, indeed, a wonderful father, but he could never satisfy her.

Once he was gone and we were alone, we sat down on the edge of the bed and waited. Our stomachs reminded us we were still alive. We each broke off a piece of the bread we had been given, though we knew it had to last a long time, maybe for days until Józio could bring us some food.

It was close to midnight when we heard footsteps approaching, a sound that was to become so familiar and dear to us that I learned to distinguish them from hundreds of others. Józio opened the door, walked in, and closed it quickly behind him. He had waited until the town was asleep before coming back to us. We were particularly concerned about our immediate neighbors. On one side of us was Gestapo headquarters; on the other the Szutpolizei (Security Police) and the Ukrainian militia. Józio's house, our shelter, was in one of the most dangerous places for Jews in all of Lesko. But because of that we hoped that no one would imagine Jews would be hiding there.

The three of us went down into the cellar and with a little shovel started digging. Unfortunately for us, this earth had been tramped on for decades making it extremely compact. It's difficult to imagine what it's like to dig in ground like that with only the smallest, flimsiest of tools. But we dug all night, until dawn. Covered with sweat and utterly exhausted, nevertheless we now had a hiding place, a hole big enough for daddy and me to push ourselves into with our faces touching the wet lime. We lay in that position all day, feeling as though we had been buried alive.

In the morning, the workshop opened. Józio and a few workers came in. The silence of the house was broken by hammering and knocking, singing and talking. Life was quite normal for every human being but a Jew.

All during the day we shivered with fear that someone might come down to the cellar. But Józio remained in the workshop all day, silently guarding the cellar door. We heard him giving orders and supervising the work as we lay silently under the floor. The tightness of the space irritated our throats but we could not utter a sound. We learned to control nature in many ways. We did not cough. It was a long, hard first day.

Finally, at seven, the workshop closed. We pushed ourselves out of the hole and straightened our bodies. Every part ached. It was agony to stretch our cramped muscles. But even more sore were our souls. Why were we doing all this? What was the purpose? Wasn't this like knocking one's head against a stone wall? But immediately another thought arose: Our child is alive. We must go on trying.

Pinek came unexpectedly that evening. He had escaped death that afternoon, having been caught at the gates of the camp carrying two blankets he intended to bring with him into hiding. After much explaining he was warned and released. In the evening he fled.

We were happy to see him although there was not as yet room for him to hide. The three of us sat down to eat a piece of bread and some water Józio had brought earlier. There were no water faucets in the house. Pinek told us about the new victims in the camp, killed during our absence.

From our family, a few were already missing: Munio, my eldest brother, and his wife and children. My oldest sister Esther and her husband, along with their daughter Sonia and son Szulo. They were liquidated with the ghetto in Sambor. My sister Hela and her husband Norbert left Lesko in November of 1941, right after the mass killing in Olszanica, in which Norbert had lost his only relative, his mother. We did not know what happened to them.

Your father's older brother David, who lived in Tarnow, had sent a man with Aryan papers meant to be used by his sisters, Hania and Sala. This gentile was to accompany the sisters and Sala's baby boy, one year old, to Tarnow. He gave them the Aryan papers but they were taken off the train between Kulawice and Yaslo. There the Gestapo took the baby from his mother and, seeing he was circumcised, smashed the baby's head against the wall. Against the same bloodstained wall, your father's sisters were shot.

Every day it seemed there were fewer and fewer people we could hope to see alive again. With each day our expectations diminished.

At this time, many families were splitting up in order to increase the chances of survival for individual members. But it wasn't easy to part. Your father wanted me to try to live on Aryan papers if we could obtain them. I could have had such a document but I didn't seize the opportunity. Dr. Lisikiewicz, daddy's friend with whom he had worked in the infirmary in Lesko during the German occupation, gave him Aryan papers for Ela, whom we didn't know at the time. (We became friendly after the liberation.) This was an opportunity to save oneself by merely changing the name and photograph on the document. I couldn't do it. We gave Ela the papers which saved her. I'm glad J had the strength at that critical time to withstand the temptation.

In the meantime, we had to work fast to make a hiding place for our dearest ones. We dug nights and rested during the days, working as silently as possible. At every sound from the street, we stopped and listened. Moreover, we now had another concern: what to do with the growing mountain of earth that became larger with each scratch we made in the dry cellar floor. How were we going to dig a hole big enough for all of us? That mountain of earth would denounce us as surely as the most vindictive and spiteful neighbors.

The loaf of bread we had from your father's last patient lasted us three days. At that time there were no more private stores in Lesko. The population received weekly rations of food and Józio wasn't prepared for additional mouths to feed. There was little in the house for his own family.

His family, of course, knew nothing about his secret undertaking to save our lives. He couldn't trust anyone, not even them, with such a secret. One slip of the tongue could cost us everything, including the lives of his own family.

We went hungry for many days but we had to continue our work and prepare a place for all of us to live for at least a few weeks. A few weeks! Józio's best estimate was that the war could not possibly last much longer than that. How short-sighted we all were. We believed in what we wished for.

We had not eaten for forty hours when we heard the angry voice of a woman above us — Józio's wife, Franciszka. She had brought his supper to the shop when he had not come home and now she was complaining bitterly. Why hadn't he fixed the part of this house that was damaged so that they could move back in here? Franka, as Józio always called her, didn't like living where she was now, in the house of a former Jewish neighbor. She was superstitious and did not want to take her things out of the house because she wanted to return to her own property.

She continued to complain in this way for a long time, while he went on working—Józio's helpers had, of course, long since gone home. He didn't seem to pay any attention to his wife. After she left he locked the door and brought his supper down to us. As always, when he appeared there was a sweet smile on his tired face. He looked at our progress approvingly and encouraged us to go on. We ate his supper as he planned further extension of our hiding place and, no matter how we pressed him, he would take none of the food for himself.

Each day brought word of the murder of more people caught in caves and forests and in hiding places around the town. At stake were not only our lives but also Józio's life and the lives of his family. But Józio was determined to share our destiny to the very end. Not only did he not repair the house but he slowly continued to destroy it, eliminating all possibility of his family moving back.

The question of where we would continue to get food was most urgent. We had to be extremely careful. At first Józio was disorganized and getting food for us was immensely difficult. He tried to take food out of his own house, but there was pitifully little and it was zealously guarded. It became a little easier when we could cook.

After four weeks of digging, our hideout was big enough to push a single cot into it, along with a little barrel for water, a hermetically sealed box for our physical needs, a little electrie stove, and a board which was added to the cot so that three could lie on it. The board also doubled as a table. In one corner we dug a canal for drainage. Józio connected the electric current to a street source so no suspicion would arise about electricity used in an empty place. The workshop was on a separate meter.

We continued to dig and enlarge the hole in hopes that the rest of the family would join us. Each morning we stopped working, covered the entrance with the board and lay there quietly until nighttime. Do you want to know how high and big this place was? It was about a meter and a half long and a meter and a half wide and high enough so that, when kneeling, our heads touched the ceiling. It became a little lower later when, for safety's sake, we made a double ceiling.

Your father always carried with him a syringe and morphine for the worst moment if we were caught. Armed with this weapon, we went on planning and preparing the hideout with more courage.

Against the part of the earth wall alongside the cot we stretched a blanket so as not to feel the wet earth when sitting there. Above us we had a tiny electric bulb which we covered with black rags so that not a ray of light shone out. That little light was our sun for almost two years. Around it revolved our dark cave life.

While the hole was still open we could go out at night, stretch and wash ourselves a little. Later that became impossible.

As I mentioned previously, water was very precious because it was so difficult for Józio to deliver anything to us, especially water. He was afraid of being seen by his neighbors. First he carried a pail of water into his stable, where he had a cow, and then he brought it into the house. After the workshop closed, he brought it down to us.

The house was a very busy place. During the day it was filled with workmen laboring above our heads; at night we continued digging the hole below. We were very exhausted and were hoping other members of the family would soon come to help us. Unfortunately and unbeknownst to us, they could no longer leave camp.

In January 1943 over 400 Gestapo and their Ukrainian helpers surrounded the sleeping camp in the early morning. The whole of the remaining group of Jews was jailed and searched. Everything was taken from them, especially knives, razor blades and tools. They remained locked up for three days and three nights without food or water and then they were pushed onto a train. That was the last transport from Zaslaw to Belzec. Peasants from nearby villages brought the news to town.

That night Józio came to see us very late. With a heavy heart and empty stomachs we waited for him until he finally opened the floor board in the black cellar above our heads and looked down at us. We looked up at him, searching for the familiar smile, but there was none.

Now, he said, you can stop digging. No one is left. We sat there in silence, stunned.

We were shocked. All our remaining families, whom we so loved, gone without a trace. Józio came down into the hole and told us what had happened in Zaslaw. We remained quiet and could not move. All those dear people gone ... disappeared ... only a memory now. We weren't hungry anymore. Our eyes were dry. We had no tears left.

Life was now nothing but despair and resignation. One envied those no longer living. They, at least, were liberated from this miserable existence. Pinek repeated constantly, "If only Milek could have survived!" Like David and Jonathan in the Bible, these two brothers had been inseparable.

Two days after the final transport had gone, about five o'clock in the morning, Józio brought Milek with him into the cellar. He opened the trap door above our heads with these words: "Milek is here." We thought we hadn't heard him correctly, that maybe we were dreaming. But it wasn't a dream.

It seemed as though he had returned from another world and we hastily pulled him in. He was pale and exhausted but unhurt from what we could see. We couldn't even speak to him, we were so overcome. It was nearly seven o'clock when the workshop would be opened.

Józio let his employees in shortly thereafter and the work began. There were so many German machines and cars to be repaired. The workmen talked above us about the liquidation of the camp and we could hear everything. Józio made believe the news didn't interest him. Hammering and singing to himself, he didn't take part in any of the gossip. Someone spoke of a group of

Jews surviving on a rocky mountain in torn rags, nearly naked, that the Gestapo was trying to catch. That evening Józio poured salt into the gasoline tanks and no one could fix the cars for three days.

The Germans thought they had a good and willing servant in Józio but what they had was a resourceful saboteur. His brother, who had come from Stanislaw and had been a high ranking officer in the Polish army, was also involved in sabotage. A niece and nephew were near starvation, but they wouldn't work for the Germans.

None, however, could match our Józio. What he did, he did without the least taint of self-interest, though he could well have profited like so many others.

Jews were not around anymore. Jewish houses and properties were sold so cheaply to the population that peasants from the countryside could do very well by taking apart the house and carting the materials away. Synagogues were also destroyed in this way. Only one, the oldest, remained, though not for sentimental reasons. No peasant wanted to touch this synagogue. The Germans were puzzled by this and tried to force a few people to pull the building apart. But some supernatural force protected every stone. One man's fingers froze, and then no one wanted to touch it. This synagogue was a few hundred years old then, and still stands today.

The old Jewish cemetery of Lesko also remained. Almost all of the Jewish cemeteries in Poland were destroyed. If human lives were not sacred, surely their remains were not respected. Some marble monuments and other valuable stones were taken away. Others were smashed and destroyed. Cemeteries were made into playgrounds, gardens and streets. The cemetery in Lesko was one of the few left intact.

We were so numb and heartbroken with the loss of the family that not even Milek's near rising from the dead could remove our depression. All day we lay motionless. In the evening, after the shop closed, we were able to feel a little relief with the outbreak of our tears.

Milek regretted bitterly that he had saved himself. He was in despair. He kept repeating over and over that he hadn't meant to save only himself. Nothing we could say comforted him.

He described in detail all that had happened after we left the camp. It had been quiet and peaceful for a time. People had more freedom to move about than before. The Gestapo left camp for the Christmas holiday. Our family was even thinking of bringing us back to the now "peaceful" camp.

Then they were surrounded unexpectedly. The evening before the round up the Gestapo chief, Kratzman, came into camp. He had new plans to rearrange Zaslaw, he said. He assured people that more work would be available for the Jews. There would have to be some preliminary shifting of people; that was all.

In the middle of the night the camp was surrounded, the people pulled out of their beds and pushed into a train. The railroad cars were so tightly packed, people were unable to breathe. The tiny windows of the cars were sealed up.

It was very sticky inside. The exhausted and thirsty people choked. There wasn't a breath of air. Soon the train started and began moving at great speed. On top of each car a guard sat with a machine gun.

Milek told us he had a piece of iron hidden in his clothes. Slowly he opened one of the little windows. A wave of cold winter air rushed into the car, cooling and refreshing the half-dead people.

Milek tried to talk other family members and people in the car into jumping out of the train with him. There was at least some chance of surviving if they tried to escape, he told them. He was sure, afterwards, that he had persuaded at least some to jump after him.

A hail of bullets whizzed past him as he fell. When he regained consciousness he found himself lying in the snow. He reached for his hat; it was riddled with bullet holes, like a sieve. He, however, wasn't hurt.

Looking around he could see there were no houses nearby and not a living soul in sight. He listened for a while and looked off into the distance. Perhaps, he thought, someone else would rise up out of the snow, someone else from the train. But his hopes were in vain.

Not knowing where he was nor in which direction to go, he picked himself up from the snow and started walking. He couldn't understand how it was possible that he was unhurt but it was a fact.

He left the tracks and walked through the fields. The snow was deep and made walking difficult. Every few minutes he stopped to breathe. He was hungry and exhausted.

After long hours of walking he stopped on the crest of a hill. His knees were buckling under him. It was sunset and it was becoming much colder. Each step in the hardened snow gave off a squeaking noise which made him afraid to proceed. He sat down. From the top of the hill he could see a village in the valley. It looked familiar. Suddenly he realized he was sitting on his own ground in our village, Orelec. He turned and saw the farmhouse where he had grown up. A shiver passed through his body.

It grew dark. No one was around. He quickly hurried toward the forest, to the remote house of the former sheriff of the town, a friend of the family before the war.

He went into his stable and lay down next to the cow to warm himself. Soon it was milking time. When the woman came into the barn and saw Milek lying near the cow she screamed and crossed herself. "Please!" Milek begged. "Don't be frightened. I mean no harm. Listen to me for a moment!" As briefly as he could, he told her what had happened and that he was trying to reach the Hungarian border. "I'll leave in just a few minutes," he promised, and asked her to send for her husband. Quieter now, she did as he asked and in a little while returned with her husband and some bread and coffee.

After a little rest and the meal, the first in four days, Milek was a little refreshed. He thanked them and left. The farmer went to the road, to make sure it was safe.

Milek walked to Lesko, a distance of 14 kilometers. He walked that whole night and reached Lesko bv sunrise. The town was still asleep. Milek went into Józio's barn to rest and warm up near his cow. Franka, Józio's wife, soon came in to milk the cow. She too was frightened. Milek repeated his story and she went to get Józio. Soon Józio came rushing into the stable with a few sheets of metal in his hands. Milek, carrying the metal sheets over his head, followed Józio into the workshop. That's how he came back to us.

By some strange coincidence what had happened to Milek paralleled, at least in part, an experience involving my father, your grandfather, less than a quarter century earlier. It was 1918, in the chaos that followed post-war, newly independent Poland. My father was on a train, on a business trip, when he was attacked by a gang of young soldiers. He was stripped of his clothes (including his fur lined coat, which must have been what attracted them) and thrown off the train. When he regained consciousness he found himself lying in the snow in his underwear and bleeding from his face and the back of his head. Shivering with cold, in terrible pain, he began walking in the blackness. After about an hour he saw a flickering light in the distance. Father walked toward it and finally, exhausted, he reached the house.

He was fortunate to have come upon a Jewish home. Father was stiff, frozen, covered with blood and mud. After explaining the circumstances, the frightened people in the house let him in. The woman made a fire and warmed some water. She washed him and helped him into bed. He remained there for three days and then returned home. I will never forget his appearance when he returned home in strange clothing, bruised and sick with pneumonia.

About you, my dear, the latest we had heard was that you were in Lwow, in the home of Wilka, Janek's fiance. We had met Wilka once for a short visit on a Sunday in Janek's house. This was before we were forced into the camp. Wilka was a tall, blonde woman, with a sweet, sincere face. I liked the location of the small house in the forest of Bezmiechowa, which Janek had taken as his home when he became the forest watchman. Janek's brother, Stefan Konkol, lived in Lesko at this time. That's how Józio found this remote cottage for you to live in as a Christian child.

Janek became attached to you. He watched you grow and play and cared for you like a father. You had a new identity. Your name was Irena Konkol. You were quickly taught to forget the names of uncles, aunts, and cousins. You were told that your parents were sent to work in Germany and you had permission to pray for their safety. They told us later that you never forgot to pray, morning or night, for the Almighty to keep your parents alive.

Janek lived with Magda, the housekeeper, and her little daughter Stasia, the same age as you. You and Stasia played and jumped like two little forest nymphs, they told us. You seemed to all outward eyes normal and carefree but at bedtime you cried for your mother. To lessen your grief your "dear Uncle Janek" tried to take my place, watching over your health and wellbeing. At night, when you had to go to the bathroom, he jumped up and lit the candle for you. Later on his love for you would stir jealousy in Magda,. She began to feel Janek was neglecting her own Stasia and there would be reproaches and quarrels. That these never led to real trouble was only because the threat hovering over all of them was so great.

This was an earlier time, however, just after the ghettos and concentration camps had been emptied. Those who had escaped death were now hunted in caves and forests. The cottage in Bezmiechowa was no longer safe and this was why he sent you to Lwow, to Wilka's house. You stayed with Wilka's family for five months. Again you were lucky and many people cared for you and kept you safe.

All this time the terrible Holocaust swept over town after town, destroying the innocent. Everywhere it was the same story, varying only in the degree of sadism demonstrated by the murderers. They came to Lwow and Wilka's family panicked. They would not allow her to keep you.

My youngest sister, Anna, had also escaped the Zaslaw camp. She had become acquainted with a young couple while working at the lumber mill with us in Lukawice. The man had expressed a desire to help her. Staszek, that was his name, talked it over with his wife and they decided to give Anna sanctuary. The general feeling among the Poles was that the end of the war was imminent. No one actually knew the truth because listening to broadcasts, especially on foreign stations, was forbidden. On December 18, the day after we had escaped the camp, Staszek was waiting outside the gates when Anna, completely muffled in clothes, emerged. He took her arm quickly and walked away with her. He brought her to his house, just beyond the mill, and she remained in hiding there. Anna stayed mainly in the cellar. When no one was around she sometimes walked through the rooms. But at the slightest noise from outside she crawled into bed and was covered up by bedding.

We knew about Anna's situation, although we had not heard from her for a very long time. Many others had tried to escape, too, but were unsuccessful. We prayed every night that Anna was still alive.

## CHAPTER FIVE
# JÓZIO - A RAY OF HOPE

**O**ur work was finished. The cellar entrance to our bunker was covered with boards and on top was a thick layer of earth. That last job Józio did; we were now locked in.

We seemed quite safe except for the sounds of the Gestapo dogs outside. When we heard a dog on the outside we would even be afraid to breathe. Whenever we slept, one of us was always on guard, to wake us if any sound was made. When the sleepers' faces became grim or sad, the one on guard woke us right away so we wouldn't make any noise that might be heard above us. Those terrible dreams of the Gestapo, of being hunted, of running in terror, continued for many years after the liberation.

The dogs were particularly terrifying. They were always at the side of the Germans. And yet, in the 22 months we were buried there, no German ever came into Józio's workshop with a dog— although many, many Germans came in. Can you understand that? If one believes in miracles, then we experienced many of them before the liberation came.

The first few weeks of mourning and despair were endless. Everything seemed to be against us. Hunger pangs were constant, and the dirt, the odor, the insects, the stickiness of the airless hole in which we huddled, all of this made some of us want to just give up. My brothers, Pinek and Milek, wanted to commit suicide and asked your father to help them do it. But he guarded the morphine very, very carefully, although he, himself, was as broken and distraught as they.

Physically I was the weakest, but I seemed to be strongest in spirit. I would not let them give up. When I look back at that time I realize that I owed that hope of survival to you. Because you were alive, for this reason alone, I was ready to suffer and live and wait and hope for a better tomorrow.

In the beginning our shelter was very cold, the earth above and around us was wet and the smell of it, the tightness of the place where we four had to live made us feel as if we were already dead. We had no water or place to wash and no change of clothing or underwear. When I saw the first insect, I wanted to scream. Pinek comforted me with the reassurance that there would be more of them. We would have to learn to like them, he said, because we would have to live with them from now on.

He was right. I had to accept the conditions. But a battle began, grim as the one against the Germans. The more insects we killed, the more came, like an organized army, in a multitude of colors and shapes. We could have supplied a research laboratory with them. The sensitivity in our fingertips became keenly developed and we could soon destroy the tiniest insects, come to feed off our bodies in the dark.

The ventilation to our living quarters was a narrow crack leading into the crowded and odoriferous cellar. Imagine how much air that provided. Breathing it was awful. The blanket with which I covered the wall began to rot and soon pieces were falling from it. Everything around us was so damp, the iron supporting our cot rusted and began to fall apart.

As a few weeks passed, we began to get used to all this, to this new way of living. Our day began at 6 A.M. I should better say our night, because when everyone else was awake and active, our rest began. We lay motionless, half sleeping, all day and into the evening when work in the shop finally stopped. Then, when everybody had gone and Józio locked the workshop door from the outside—which never happened until 8 P.M.—our "day" began. This was our winter schedule. In the summer it was much worse. The workdays in the shop were endless in summer and that meant greater danger and greater suffering. Even on Sundays, in the summer, the workmen came into the shop.

Next to safety, the question of food was our most urgent concern. Józio had to handle the shop and many family problems; we were an additional four mouths to feed. He walked around in a daze. He didn't have the time or opportunity to think how to cope with all the problems. There was no one with whom he could discuss things either. He was joined together with us, for life or for death. Finding food under these conditions was no easy problem to solve.

Our food supply for the first four or five weeks was a few potatoes he had managed to sneak out of his home. But there was so little food there that Franka immediately noticed if anything was missing. She often asked the children what was happening to the food she had brought. This way of supplying us was very dangerous and inadequate; it also didn't supply us with more than a small bite every 40 hours. And so we balefully saw each other fading away. We became pale, yellow, skinny. Our eyes deepened and our faces aged daily.

We tried to persuade Józio to go to the countryside and buy flour and barley from the peasants. In the beginning he was reluctant to do this, afraid he might arouse suspicion. He was even afraid to buy a newspaper, or writing paper, pencils or books. Those things would have been a great blessing for us but he was very careful and we could not ask him to take even greater risks on our behalf.

But we had to find something to occupy our minds or go mad. In our misery, time seemed not to move. Nature stood still. Was it a test to see how much we could withstand?

In the long, dark hours each of us tried to occupy our minds. We reviewed our past and dreamed about the future. We thought about good food and restaurants. When one is very hungry the first thought and the last is about food.

Milek was often counting. He got himself lost in numbers. Pinek recited psalms and poetry. Whatever one had read or heard was repeated.

What we missed most was the opportunity to write. The most primitive things, like light and a flat surface, were wanting. Our little light was very tiny indeed, shining through the dark cover. After the town was asleep, we would turn it on and life for us began. We washed as best we could, we clustered round the light, we tried to straighten our backs. Personal hygiene was difficult, as you can imagine. We washed our hands and I peeled a few potatoes from which I made what was to us a delicious soup. No meal had ever tasted so good to us. We couldn't wait until it was ready. The little electric stove was next to the cot, near us, the only dry place in our "home."

Once we gave up a few potatoes for a chess set. We carved little chess figures and dried them until they were hard as stone and made a chess board from a piece of plywood. This helped pass the time.

Our hole, which was so cold in the beginning, got hotter all the time. We lay in our underwear. The rest of our clothing we used as pillows under our heads. They were practically rotten anyway. The boys hardly worried about it. The things people concern themselves with in normal life were not our concerns. We didn't worry about clothing, about bathing—we hardly had enough water to drink so there could be no talk of such a luxury. The men didn't wash or change their clothes the whole 22 months we were trapped there. They didn't shave or cut their hair. They were quite interesting to look at.

My vanity as a woman compelled me to act differently. From our daily quart of shared water, I always spared a few drops to wash my face. I did this daily, with whatever liquid I had, whether water or a few drops of buttermilk. I washed my face and combed my hair and, also, once in a few weeks, not listening to my brothers, I spared a little water to wash around my body—in the dark of course.

They made fun of me, the way I hoped and prepared myself to live. My only dress, in which I had escaped from the camp, hung over the tiny electric kitchen where it was dry and covered for preservation. It was wrapped in a rag and carefully watched by me so my dress and shoes became objects of a little fun on my account. I was glad.

Franka, Józio's wife, became more and more suspicious of the mysterious disappearance of potatoes, bread and many things she prepared. She asked her husband but he pleaded innocence, of course. She made inquiries among the children, he told us later. She asked them to keep watch, especially during her absences and to watch their father, in particular. She investigated among the neighbors and asked them to aid her in solving the mystery. Her relentless suspicions began to threaten our lives with discovery.

She started to visit the workshop each day and demanded that Józio finish repairing the house so the family could move back. It seemed strange and suspicious to her that the house appeared more damaged with each day. This made her frantic because the property was hers, her inheritance. She didn't like living in a Jewish home and felt no Jewish house could substitute for her own.

Then a new thought came to her mind. Her husband, she concluded, must be supporting another woman, though she couldn't imagine who. Her search now gained momentum. Once the suspicion had entered her thoughts, her imagination would not rest. Neither we nor Józio guessed at the time just how much danger we were all in because of her suspicions.

Her spying on him became quite extensive, and she asked the Ukrainian police to put her neglectful and philandering husband under surveillance to right the wrong she believed was being done to her and her children. Once aroused, she was like a demon. We became afraid that Józio would make some slip and she would find us out.

Józio was amazing, however. He played two entirely different roles. At home he looked dissipated and disorganized, never quite clean, stubble on his face, seemingly unable to maintain either himself or his family, or even his home, in anything like good order. Yet in his shop, in regard to us, he worked with precision and skill.

He really didn't care about his appearance, nor about the amenities of house, family and personal comfort—and this was the greatest possible protection we could have had. No one could have connected this preoccupied workman, his hands and face invariably flecked with grease, with any subversive activities. With his seemingly uncaring attitude he projected the image of someone proficient enough in work to be useful to the Germans and yet apparently shiftless; a good natured, hardworking lout any German could treat with benign contempt.

But he noticed everything, registered every change in the situation—in town, in the countryside, among the Germans, in the shop—anything that might possibly affect us. He was, with heart and soul and every fiber of his being, concerned—both with his friends and his enemies. If his wife was persistent and devious in her endless snooping, he was ten times more clever than she. He would never make a move that might reveal our presence until he was absolutely sure he was not observed.

He juggled an amazing number of things in that dear, disheveled head of his. He was concerned about you. He was in contact with Anna, living in Stascek's house—and many other people as well. He knew about them but they, at the time, did not know about us. Józio was the only person who knew about us—our only connection with the outside world.

He was also connected with the Polish underground. He was their courier and illegal postman. He carried their letters and news of underground activities between the groups. It's hard to believe that he was able to keep each of these involvements separate and still play the casual role of father (he loved his children deeply) and husband and all the while avoid discovery. His days were one long exertion—his energy immeasurable.

Of course we didn't know of his many activities at that time. But each morning, when we heard his steps approaching the house, we thanked God.

It was easier at first, when Józio kept the family cow in the stable in back of the workshop. He had a reason then to carry water and other things back and forth—some of which he later brought down to us. Afterwards, because Franka decided she could not rely on him to tend the cow, she began to come to the stable herself, which made it much harder for us.

Józio worked for the Gestapo, fixing their cars and trucks and also worked for the local dairy company, repairing their machinery when it broke down. For this he was sometimes given cheese, butter or milk. He would invariably bring these "bonuses" to us. We protested that he should take these things home to his children, but he insisted we at least take part for ourselves. We needed it more than the children, he said, because they were outside in the sunlight and fresh air.

He was like a kind and tender father to us, and he was particularly good to me. He decided that I especially was the most delicate and least likely to survive our underground ordeal and so, each time he came, as he lay on the floor looking down at us through the hole, he insisted that I come closer to the opening so he could get a good look at me. He had the idea that I, as a woman, would be more delicate than the men and at more risk.

More than with food, we were fed with the good news Józio always brought—news from the front. He brought us good news even when there was none, just to lift our spirits. The little hope sustained us like a nourishing dinner. But the hoped-for victory approached at a turtle's pace and the misery and despair of our daily lives continued.

Our library consisted of a few books Józio had found in the street and brought down to us. We had Schiller and a few books in Hebrew, among them a book of the Prophet Daniel, which speaks of the Messiah. We read each of the books hundreds of times, but the book of Daniel we studied with such care it practically disintegrated in our hands.

This book says that before the Messiah will come there will be awful times for the Jews. There will be such destruction that only one in a family, two in a town, will remain. It seemed to us that the time of the Messiah had come.

Our hole was hot, but outside it was a hard, frosty Polish winter. We couldn't see it but we recreated it in our minds: the snow, the trees, the icicles gleaming in the sunlight—the whole beautiful vista of nature in winter which I had loved so much. We could hear the sounds of walking on frosty snow and the sound of the wind.

Because Franka had long wanted to move back into her own house but was frustrated that Józio wouldn't repair the place, and was, in fact, slowly demolishing it, she at last gave up and decided the cow had to be moved to the new house as well. Now Józio had to use all his ingenuity to get us water. He visited many houses while carrying his pail of water so that Franka and her spies could not determine which house he visited most frequently. Nevertheless, Franka picked a victim. One of the houses Józio visited belonged to a middle-aged spinster, a school teacher. This was the guilty party, Franka decided, the one leading Józio astray. All her anger and bitterness were directed at this woman. When it became clear, even to Franka, that she was not the imagined villainess, Franka searched for a new focus for her suspicions. She was sure she would find her husband's mysterious lover eventually.

In the long hours of darkness I reviewed my life, my home. I escaped into the happy recollections I still had of my childhood on the farm. Before my eyes stood the erect figure of my father, strict with us but also gentle and loving. He never punished us physically. It wasn't necessary because we had immense respect for him and obeyed him in everything. The sound of his steps in the hall was enough to interrupt our mischief.

He had been a wise and busy man, often called upon to mediate and counsel disputes in business or in private relationships. From his early youth he had worked hard to support himself and his elderly parents. My grandmother was fifty years old when my father, the youngest of her children, was born. He was nineteen when he married my mother, Rachel Trenk, the gentlest of women. Her world was her home and her ten children,whom she raised with all the anxious care and immense love of a Jewish mother.

But home and family weren't her only concerns. There was also the wider "family," the poor, the needy and the sick in our town. Our community, as everywhere in Poland and Eastern Europe, did not have an organized welfare organization to help the sick and indigent. My mother was known for her charitable work. She dispensed food, money and clothing. She told no one where she went. She knew where every old and sick person lived and made sure that whatever was given by others would reach those for whom it was intended as soon as possible. At harvest time she saw to it that the potatoes, vegetables, grain and wood were delivered promptly and in the largest possible quantities to the needy.

My mother also had an artistic nature. She loved to knit and embroider. We had closets filled with sweaters and shawls that she had made. For two years she embroidered and prepared my trousseau, but she did not live to see my wedding.

I was engaged to be married to your father in 1932. He was in his senior year of medicine in Prague, at the German University, because it was very difficult for a Jew to study medicine in Poland. Once, when he came home for summer vacation, we met and became engaged. It was a happy time. Our family was close-knit and loving. We enjoyed life. Your father and I explored the woods, swam in the cold mountain spring, fished, and rode horseback.

On winter vacations there was also fun: snowball fights, sledding, skiing. I can remember startling your father's parents late on a Saturday night when we suddenly appeared in the frosty moonlight on skis, holding onto a rope behind a horse-drawn sled. It had been an exhilarating ride on that crisp, moonlit evening.

In 1933 your father completed his studies in Prague and came home. We wanted very much to marry but it seemed impossible at the moment. Mother wasn't well. My oldest brother had married and moved away, followed by my two older sisters. I was now the oldest living at home and many of the responsibilities of caring for the family now fell on me.

Still, we felt if we could not marry at once we could at least plan our future life together. This was a time when many young Jews became ardent Zionists and began planning to immigrate to Palestine. We too hoped to make our home there.

After my mother was feeling better, we turned to our parents to discuss this plan, seeking their approval. We added a further, more practical reason: your father had his diploma in medicine from the German University of Prague but he was still far from being able to practice if he remained in Poland. For that he had to pass the Polish State Boards examination which would take even more time.

But both his parents and mine could not see why we were in such a hurry to leave Poland. Wait, they counseled, take the State Board examinations first and then, if you still want to go, you will have our blessings.

So your father registered for the examinations in Lwow and went there to study. I remember going there to visit him. His roommate was Dr. Glinert and both of them worked hard, week after week, never taking a day off from their books.

When I came I found him working so hard the sweat shone on his face. He was a very ambitious student and finished far ahead of his colleagues, astonishing the examiners with how quickly he was able to finish his boards. He then became an intern in one of the bigger hospitals in Warsaw.

I can hear you saying that now we should have gone to Palestine. The answer is that I couldn't. My sister Clarisse was ill and Mother, whose health had become uncertain, took her illness very badly. We now had two seriously ill patients on our hands. Slowly Clarisse recovered, but mother died in the early spring of 1935.

Again I had to take her place at home as much and as often as I was able. My brother-in-law Sam, Clarisse's husband, who was, like the rest of us, deeply attached to my mother, came home from Italy saddened, as I had never seen him before. When the funeral was over he took Clarisse with him to Italy to allow her to fully recover, both from her own illness and from mother's death. She helped him make a living while he finished his medical studies there.

Five years had passed since your father and I had met and decided to become man and wife. And still we weren't married. We determined in our letters back and forth from Warsaw that we would wait no longer. And as soon as your father had a vacation from the hospital, we were married.

Our wedding was small and quiet, not at all like the elaborate weddings my older sisters and brother had had when my mother was still alive.

We moved into our new apartment and opened an office in Sanok. And we gave up the idea of going to Palestine. My father, your grandfather, was struggling hard to be both parents to the remaining children at home, but it was impossible. His role had always been outside the home; he could not remake himself now. Someone had to help him. I felt that I couldn't leave.

Your father quickly found his place among the physicians of the town—the senior doctors at least. There were 20 physicians in town and, although your father was known and liked, even before opening an office in Sanok many of these doctors objected to the innovations in diagnosis and treatment that your father introduced.

The senior physicians, like Dr. Ramer and Dr. Hertzik, more independent and more forward looking than the others, joined in consultation with your father. They had begun to like him very much and to trust his judgment. After a few months, with their help, the opposition from the others largely collapsed and your father became fully accepted by his colleagues; he was already widely known and very much liked by the townspeople. We were all—my father and daddy's family—delighted with his success.

Two years had passed since my mother's death. One day your grandfather came to see us to "consult" with me about an important matter. He wanted to remarry.

My stepmother, Sarah, was a good, if slightly foolish lady who soon found a thousand slights and indignities being inflicted upon her by her husband's children. She never failed to tax him with them. Nevertheless we were on good terms.

Time passed, we were settled now in our marriage and home in Poland. We hardly thought any longer of our dream of going to Palestine.

All these things consumed me as I lay with the others in the blackness of our hole underneath the workshop. The men tramped and whistled and worked away over our heads—and I lay there remembering my childhood, the farm, the childish troubles we had with the tutors who lived with us during the long winters.

The past came back to me in vivid waves of remembrance, so painful to think of and yet so dear. For a little while such memories comforted me and then the awful thought: "All these people are dead."

In the close, fetid air of our hole I was chilled to my bones.

The noises above us subsided and the closing of the lock on the workshop door interrupted my reveries. In the silence we stretched and began to speak.

CHAPTER SIX

# LIFE IN A RAT HOLE

We turned on the dim little light and the routine of personal cleanliness began. We washed our hands with a few drops of very precious water. You must know that the cow was no longer in the stable. Franka had moved her away, nearer to her home. From that moment, the delivery of water and food had become ever more dangerous, and the quantity we were provided grew smaller and smaller.

For Józio the constantly increasing difficulties were a source of seemingly unbearable pressure. We gave him the little money we had managed to hold on to and encouraged him to buy flour, barley or potatoes. He was reluctant because he was afraid.

As time went on, things improved a little. Józio became a little calmer. He seemed to have gained a greater ability to cope with the situation. He managed to get us a little flour and then, for his work in the dairy, he got a few pounds of butter and brought some to us. I boiled it down and put it into jars for preservation.

No stores were open in Lesko during the whole occupation. Lesko was a border town, first occupied by the Russians, then the Germans. Food was rationed by the authorities. One could only buy extra food from peasants in the surrounding villages, but it was hard for Józio to leave his workshop in search of food.

The little bit of flour we had was soon gone. The butter was all we had for days at a time. We licked the butter in the jars. Some time later Józio managed to buy a sack of barley. The butter was all gone now but the barley tasted wonderful, even without the butter, and lasted a long time. We had a meal every day and began to look better. When the barley ran out, Józio brought us some potatoes.

Not long after we closed the hole we realized that we were not going to eat our meals alone. There were other hungry creatures in the hole. The smell of boiling potatoes attracted mice. They, too, received their portions at every meal for they were not kind enough to leave until they had eaten. More and more of these visitors came, until one day we noticed a new creature among them. He was standing in the crevice in the wall, looking at us as if to say "What are you doing in my territory?" He was the size of a small cat, with brown fur and a thick tail, like that of a mink. Oh, how frightened I was. The men were very worried too, though they concealed it a little better.

We were afraid our new visitor would bring others and that they would dispossess us, digging away at our home until we were visible to the people above us.

That rat became our constant companion, but he never brought his friends to dinner. He encircled our hole with tunnels but, after he had made his access easy, he stopped digging. Every evening, when he smelled food, he joined our little group and waited with us. He never failed to join us at mealtime and, when he had received his portion, he quietly departed.

We waited anxiously each day for the evening to arrive because each evening Józio stopped by to see us for a few minutes. The news he brought one evening was especially exciting; a friend had given him a short-wave radio and as long as he already had "illegal stuff" under the cellar floor he thought he might as well have a radio too.

The population was forbidden to listen to radio broadcasts. Even possession of a short-wave was punishable by death.

We were very excited by the idea of listening to first-hand news and looked forward to having the radio in our hole. The next morning Józio brought it into the workshop in a wheelbarrow, covered by a sack. That evening he pushed the receiver into the hole.

Józio gave us two sets of earphones and Milek, who was technically proficient, had soon rigged the receiver so we could hear with no sound escaping. The long hours we had to endure in the dark were suddenly transformed.

That radio changed our lives. Each of us had one ear- phone from the two sets. We listened to from twelve to fourteen newscasts each day. We listened to local Polish stations, then Berlin, Moscow and London. Whatever else happened to us—increased danger, periods of near starvation, all the rest of it—we felt restored to human existence by that radio. It alternately filled us with hope and then tremendous despair and anxiety as we followed the strategies of the fighting forces on the front.

Each evening, after the shop closed, we discussed the daily news. Each successful move of the Russians made us happy; every German counterattack filled us with despair. On the whole, there was more despair than hope.

We heard the newscasts in many languages: Polish, German, Russian and Ukrainian. We heard newscasts from London—spoken in the Polish language. The Germans were boasting of their victories and the Polish government-in-exile in London was broadcasting German defeats and announcing the coming of the Allies and the second front. We had already heard about that second front and we waited for it impatiently. The thought that it might happen soon enough for us to survive was so overwhelming we could hardly bear it. As time passed, and there was still no Allied invasion of German-occupied Europe, we began increasingly to despair.

We were hungry all the time. At any moment something could happen—Józio might not be able to get food to us, something could happen to him—and we would die. The news on the radio made us feel our situation all the more sharply.

Spring came. More and more people were murdered on the streets of Lwow, people pulled out of forests and caves and other hideouts and slaughtered in the streets. The ghetto was emptied of every last soul. You were then in Lwow but Janek's future in-laws were afraid to keep you. You had been with them for five months.

Because Józio had begged him to, and because he knew it was necessary, Janek went to Lwow to get you. I can only imagine how you must have felt and what kind of an impact those frequent changes of place and people had on you. Janek had learned that a number of people knew of your existence and he was advised to turn you over to the Germans quickly, before he, his family and his future bride's family were killed. Józio, however, convinced Janek and the others to remain silent and keep you safe.

The area of the forest where Janek lived had now been declared *Judenrein*—clean of Jews. As such, the Germans were no longer searching intensively there. Józio begged Janek to keep you and care for you, promising to help him with expenses. He told him your parents were alive and he'd be responsible for anything that happened to you. Józio's words and Janek's devotion to you prevailed over the pressure that his father and brother had put on him to do away with you.

You were now sharing Janek's cabin in the forest again. We hoped you would be happy there. Janek was the forest watchman, rifle on shoulder. You and Stasia and the dog would run after him in the woods. We hoped the beautiful surroundings would help you forget a little of the sorrows of which you could not speak.

How did I know so much about you? From Józio. He visited you and brought back reports of what you did and what you said, each word of which I would dwell on and embroider in my mind in the long dark night of our concealment.

I knew, for instance, that there was a little spring near the house where you and Stasia, who was your age, would wash yourselves and play. You picked flowers in the field and berries in the forest and brought them home. And I knew that the fresh air and sunshine made you look brown and healthy as any normal child.

Józio had brought us a drawing you had made. It was a drawing of a cat, made with one expressive line. Completely on your own, without anyone showing you how, you had begun to draw. You drew people, houses, animals and trees. Janek was amazed at your talent. I cherished the little drawing but I had to be careful about taking it out to look at because each time a little of it disappeared off the paper.

I had something else equally precious: a photo of you. Janek had been a photographer in Posen before the war. When the Germans took Posen and confiscated his property he came to our region and became a forest watchman. I understood that he had taken many photos of you.

There was not a waking hour of the day or night that I did not thank God for preserving you. You were our hope. Every word about you, transmitted through Józio, gave us energy in our fight for survival. Apart from these thoughts and little keepsakes I had from you, our lives continued to be a torment. There was no relief possible, not even a sob, a cough or a sneeze. Any uttered sound could mean our deaths.

Pinek was very uncomfortable too. He often complained. Your father and Milek complained the least. They took everything like saints, they were so heroic.

But with all that, the food problem was still worse—there was almost nothing.

One night Józio didn't come to see us as he usually did. We couldn't imagine what had happened to him. A long, anxious night followed and our attention was fixed upon listening for his steps when he came to open the shop in the morning. The shop opened but Józio wasn't there. The workers seemed to be alone.

We listened intently for any talk about him but his name was never mentioned. The usual knocking and hammering went on all day but there was no sign of Józio or even a member of his family. We didn't see him that evening either. We were frantic by then and couldn't think of anything that would keep him from us like this for two days. We knew Józio. Only a catastrophe could have kept him away.

We couldn't wait for morning, praying that he would open the shop as usual. We were like animals in a cage—completely dependent on our keeper, waiting to be fed. Józio was our lifeline, the one and only person who knew of our existence. Without him we would cease to be. Our feverish imaginations pictured scenes of Józio having been caught by the Germans. Perhaps he had not been careful enough distributing newscasts, perhaps he had been caught with forbidden equipment, perhaps someone else knew about us now?

The third day arrived and, again, the shop was opened but without Józio. Now we were really panicky. We were sure the worst had happened and soon Józio's fate would overtake us. We couldn't think clearly but we had to make a decision for the approaching night. If possible, we had to wait until the middle of the night and go out into the forest. We hadn't eaten for three days and there was no water to drink. We were too weak to make any decision and even weaker for carrying it out. The insects were awfully bad by then ... or maybe we had just weakened too much to fight them.

Finally the evening arrived and there was no sign of Józio. To avoid losing out minds, we tried to distract ourselves. We began to talk about you and the amazing things you used to say and do. We poked fun at one another's appearance. Most of the time I was the object of the jokes ... the way I tried to preserve my dress in which I hoped to walk out free again when this was all over, the way I cared about my face and combed my hair. We talked about all the things and deeds that one was either bitter or glad about. We mentioned all the good foods we had tasted in our lives and, at the end, we had a game of chess for dessert! After it all, we put our tired heads down on the hard cot and tried to sleep and dream of Józio's coming back, at last, the following day.

On the fourth day of this ordeal he finally arrived ... and all in one piece. He had been delayed by a series of adventures which began when he hired himself out to a peasant to work for some grain. Afterwards, he'd been busy delivering the underground mail and the newspapers. Our joy at his arrival is indescribable. He was back, that was all we knew or cared about! And he'd brought with him flour, barley and marmalade—enough to last us a couple of weeks.

In all of Poland at that time only three ghettos were left, in Lodz, Krakow and Warsaw. In all other cities, towns and villages, throughout the entire country, no Jews remained. There were still some living among the gentiles, with Aryan papers and, perhaps a few scattered here and there living underground like us.

The newspapers, in both Polish and German, announced the news each time another poor victim was caught. Prizes were offered for their capture but a Jewish head was worth very little: three hundred zlotys a head—the price of a pound of butter. For the head of an exceptional Jew, like Professor Einstein, the reward was 500 zlotys. Józio brought us back a newspaper where the prize announcements were made. The newspaper article proclaimed that Jews would no longer celebrate their holiday of Purim in any nation in Europe.

What they meant, Rena, was this: In the old story of Purim, Haman, the prime minister of the Persian king, aimed to destroy the Jewish people within Persia on a single day. But when Xerxes, the Persian king, learned this would include the slaughter of his own wife, Esther, herself a secret Jew, he altered the decree Haman had issued in his name, giving Jews the opportunity to defend themselves at the moment of attack. Hitler wanted to suggest that it was the Jews' plan, all along, to destroy the non-Jews of Europe as they had once defeated their enemies in ancient Persia and that he was the one who would prevent this by his policies of suppression and murder. Of course we had been listening to German radio stations night after night, so this report in the newspaper came as no surprise. We had heard it all before.

The German newscasts at this time spoke about their victories on the Russian front but foreign communiques denied these and reported deep Russian penetration into German lines. Who knew what to believe? London kept repeating that the Allied invasion would soon take place. The knowledge that you were still alive and well gave us all hope despite the confusion of events.

I don't think I could have lasted as long as I did in that hole without this knowledge. The conditions we were surviving under affected me even more than the others. The inability to maintain personal hygiene was especially awful. None of the others were comfortable in that dirt-walled tomb—how could they have been? —but for me, especially, it was a living hell. Although I washed myself more than they did—using up more of our precious water— it was never enough. I was plagued by terrible itching because of the overall conditions of the hole: the dirt, the poor nutrition and avitiminosis, and lack of air and sunlight. My fingertips were swollen from scratching. My blood vessels were weak and broke easily, causing frequent bleeding under the skin. My arms and legs were covered with black spots.

The itching lasted for months but this wasn't even the worst of it. I had developed an allergy or maybe it was a cold. My nose was clogged and I couldn't breathe easily. Your father would wave a piece of plywood over my face like a fan to help me.

We listened night after night to the clandestine Polish station Kosciuszko and began to hear about the uprising of the Jews in the Warsaw Ghetto. The station was appealing to the Polish population to help the Jews who were fighting the Germans there. We listened to reports of the heroic fight the men, women and children in the Ghetto put up for forty-two days. They were hoping the free world would come to help them. But the newscasts about the plight of the Jews in Warsaw continued to worsen. The appeal to the world, an appeal that was heartbreaking in its intensity and which should have moved the world to action seemed, incredibly, to go unheeded. Radio Moscow called on the Poles in the underground to help the resistance in Warsaw. They must be blind not to see their own interests in this fight, the commentators said repeatedly. One small group of the underground did respond— the Armia Ludowa, the Communists. A committee had also been formed in London to help the Jews in Poland, but elsewhere, among the allies, there was almost no response. Whatever meager efforts were mounted, they were all too late.

One night I will never forget. It was May 1, 1943. We heard a broadcast of a kind we had never heard before. From the radio in our hole came the voice of Szmul Zigelbaum, a leader in the Jewish socialist underground organization known as the Bund. He spoke in Polish from London where the organization was based and directed his words to us, to the Jews in holes, in ghettos, wherever we might be found. All the time we had been living under the ground, we hadn't known if the world was even aware of us, of what was happening to us. Did they know we were being hunted like animals? How we were hiding, trying to survive in the most terrible circumstances, fearing every minute for our lives?

That night Zigelbaum spoke to us: "Jews in the forests," he said, "Jews in the caves, Jews hiding in holes in the earth, we know you are there. You are not alone. The world knows about your suffering and is coming to help you. They must come. Wherever you are, wherever you can hear me, you must live. The world knows. Strengthen your spirit and live."

So he spoke, from his heart. Oh, how we cried. This was the first time anything concerning our plight had been broadcast on the radio.

But his plea for help for the fighting Warsaw Ghetto went unheeded. The Nazis were bombing the Ghetto and it was in flames. When the six-week long battle ended, and with it all our hopes, Mr. Zigelbaum, in great desperation and in protest, committed suicide in the House of Parliament in London.

We lay desperate and bitter in our hole, convinced that nothing would be done until not a single Jew remained alive. With the destruction of this ghetto, the last vestige of Jewish life as we had known it in Poland had vanished. The disappointment we felt over the inaction of the free world, their utter silence, was unbearable. The Warsaw Ghetto's heroic effort was over and their heartbreaking cry had been in vain.

Our own chances of survival grew poorer each day, although Radio Moscow gave very good reports about their fighting forces and promised that the Allied invasion would soon become a reality. But our belief in the possibility of our own survival faded. The second front would not come soon enough to save us.

During the winter, Józio had gone to visit you at Janeks and came away much perturbed because you didn't seem to be dressed warmly enough for the cold weather. He found a ball of wool yarn which his wife had put away to use for a sweater for one of the children and took it to my sister Anna, then hiding in Lukawice, in Staszeks house near the lumber mill. She knitted a sweater for you. The resultant commotion at home made his life, and all our lives, harder still. Franka was now absolutely convinced that Józio had another woman. Her search for this woman became an obsession and it's a miracle she never learned the truth until the eve of the liberation.

This was the kind of thing Józio did. He was so careful in everything he said and did to protect us, yet his care for us and his lack of concern for himself constantly put all of us in danger, as when he brought us the radio from the Polish underground, which was too large to be easily concealed. Yet Józio, in his enthusiasm, risked certain death by bringing it to his shop in midday in a wheelbarrow. He ran around coughing and sneezing and often feverish with bad colds. Once he came to us bruised all over—he had fallen off the roof while trying to repair it. We always worried about him. But nothing we said would make him take better care of himself. We only learned much later that, besides his family, his workshop and the secret burden of our existence, he was serving as a courier for the underground.

In a sense, dear Rena, your mother, father and uncles were all actively engaged in the resistance because, through Józio, we shared the information we gathered from the daily newscasts we monitored from London, Moscow and Berlin. We were among the first people in the world to hear of the German defeat and the surrender of the Nazi general Paulus at Stalingrad. The initial reports stated that the Nazis had suffered 100,000 casualties and that 300,000 were taken prisoner. This gave us hope that the tide of battle had finally turned.

On another occasion we had heard a voice we believed was Stalin's urging soldiers and the general population to defend Moscow at all costs.

But Russian victories at the front did not necessarily mean good news for the surviving Jews. The Nazi timetables for our extermination were simply speeded up. Gestapo actions now had priority over the military for the use of equipment and transportation needed to facilitate extermination of Jews. Retreating armies were instructed to burn mass graves and the huge piles of bodies left in camps and ghettos. Our neighbor Usher Schwartz was among a group of seventy Jews spared from the last transport to Belzec to be put to work burning and destroying the evidence of what had occurred in the Zaslaw camp between 1941 and January of 1943. After the liberation, when Russian soldiers, advancing toward the West arrived, we learned of the charred remains of the mass graves. Captain Leibowicz of the Russian army was most informative.

The long winter, which we had not been able to see, passed and it was spring again outside. We could hear birds singing in the quiet of the dawn. According to the calendar it was now Passover, the holiday of freedom. We recalled for one another how we had celebrated this festival in days past at home, the long, beautifully set Seder table with the whole family around it; my parents, the children and grandchildren...Sonia, Szulo, Alek. We talked about all of them, lingering lovingly over each detail. This present Passover we felt we were suffering even more than the afflictions that befell our ancestors, for we were condemned not merely to slavery but to death.

This Passover eve Józio, quite unexpectedly, brought us a loaf of bread he had gotten from the Nazis. It was our first bread since we went into hiding, December 1, 1942. What a paradox, that bread should arrive from our oppressors on the eve of Passover. It gave us special pleasure as we partook of our feast, that this, the bread of affliction had been taken from our enemy.

When the summer finally arrived, we were in greater danger of discovery than before. Working hours were now from dawn until sunset, with more frequent visits from the Gestapo. As I said before, we were fortunate they never brought their dogs into Józio's shop or we would have most certainly been found out. The conditions in the hole became unbearable. The heat, the smell, the lice, the itching and our increased need for the nearly unavailable water made this the most difficult time.

Then, in August 1943, we suddenly heard that Mussolini had been overthrown in Italy. The announcement was repeated many times on foreign newscasts and we regained a little hope. Perhaps the war really was coming to an end. Once again we summoned up what strength we still had to continue our fight to survive.

We discussed with Józio the possibilities of getting food. We discussed how we would manage when the front came closer and our electricity would inevitably be cut off. Our survival had become dependent on the little hotplate on which I cooked our potatoes. We expected rapid developments on the front and further breakthroughs into German occupied territories. Józio brought us a map and the boys dug in and became experts in the strategy of the fighting forces. It was a pity no one asked their opinion. Still, it strengthened our morale.

We could only live for a certain amount of time on encouraging events, however. As time passed and our liberation seemed as far away and as unlikely as ever, our mood changed. Once more there were long hours ... days, nights, weeks, months of endless discomfort and privation, of hunger and despair.

My sister Anna, who was in hiding, hadn't heard from us in a year and became so worried that she took a chance by asking Staszek, in whose house she was hiding, to find out if we were still alive. This meant telling him about our hideout, but she was desperate to know.

And so one Sunday afternoon, when there was no one in the shop, we heard the door open and two people come in. We heard Józio lock the door on the inside and talk to someone as they walked into the kitchen. We were taken aback and very frightened.

Crouched in our hole we waited, as Józio lifted the floor-board, lay down and looked inside at us. He said Staszek was with him and would like to see us in order to bring personal regards to Anna. Józio carefully explained that Anna had insisted Staszek confirm our continued existence with his own eyes.

Then Staszek, himself, looked through the hole. He looked strained and worried when he saw us and expressed sympathy with our living conditions, which must have seemed as horrible to him as they felt to us. He told us he hoped to celebrate the victory over the Nazis together with us when the time came and asked that I, specifically, come closer to the opening in the floor so he could get a good look at me. It was one of the things he had promised Anna he would do: to tell her how I looked. He looked for a long time at my face and was very kind. He said I looked far better than he had expected, in fact rather attractive, he assured me, and the compliment pleased me, whether it was true or not. We had a good conversation that Sunday afternoon and even discussed whether he might help Józio find food for us. We sent our love to his wife and to Anna and then he left, deeply shaken.

But it frightened us more now, that someone else should know where we were. It increased the chances of our being discovered. We had made great efforts to ensure there were no connections between the hiding places of our different family members or of our friends. If any of us were captured, there would be grave consequences for all. Your father and I were particularly upset because this made your hiding place more vulnerable.

As I've already mentioned, Staszek and his wife had hidden Anna in his employee's cottage at the lumber mill where he worked in Lukawice. Although living in much better circumstances than ours, she was in constant danger there. If something turned up missing from the mill or anything went wrong, there were sudden, unannounced searches of all the cottages, making Anna vulnerable. Visits from neighbors, who might come by at any time, were equally risky. Because of this, Staszek and his wife were rarely at home. Anna remained locked in an apparently empty house. When Staszek went to work, his wife, Victoria, visited relatives and friends and didn't return until late at night.

To guard against being seen from the windows, Anna spent the daylight hours concealed in a bed under heavy quilts and pillows. Although she lived in constant fear, she was still better off than we were, however, because she was able to read or knit sometimes. You'll recall, Rena, that she knit a sweater for you with the wool Józio had brought her.

In the spring of 1944, fear of a sudden search became a reality. The main transmission belt at the mill was stolen. There was an uproar and the Gestapo began the systematic searches of every house in the area. When he heard the belt was missing, Staszek removed Anna from the house and brought her to where you were staying in Janek's cottage in the forest of Bezmiechowa. (At that time he already knew where you were hidden.)

But now there was another problem. Anna assumed another identity when she came to Bezmiechowa. She called herself "Miss Stefa," a Polish lady who was a friend of the family. But you recognized her. You recognized her teeth, her smile, even the sweater she wore and she had to continually convince you that she was not your Aunt Anna but someone else.

You dared not ask questions but were drawn to her and you watched her. You saw that whenever a stranger was about she hid herself and that she kept apart from the family, slept in the barn and spent most of her time there. When you were alone you sneaked into the barn to have a chat with Miss Stefa. She couldn't resist kissing and hugging you. Once when you weren't well you even asked her to sit with you. She sponged you down to relieve your high fever and kissed you on the chest. You were amazed. You told her that only your mother had ever kissed you on that place and, because she looked so much like your aunt, was it possible that she was? No, she was not your aunt, she replied, crying the whole time.

Anna stayed with you for five or six weeks. During that time, Staszek was arrested and jailed for two months, charged with sabotage at work. Many were questioned and arrested. Józio told us he was afraid this search for the transmission belt would uncover all of us. Janek became afraid to keep Anna with him any longer and Józio brought her to us.

From the time of Mussolini's fall we waited impatiently for the coming of the Second Front and the Nazis defeat. But months passed and it just didn't happen. Finally, one year after Mussolini's demise, we learned at last, from the radio, that the Allies had landed in France. With tears of happiness pouring down our cheeks we listened to the recurrent radio bulletins describing the spectacular landing of the Americans on the coast of Normandy in June 1944. We were so very sorry that all of our loved ones had not lived to hear this with us. We were certain now that the war would soon be over and even made bets about how far off our liberation now was.

We began to make preparations for the coming of the Russian Front. It would be a critical time for us. From bits of flour I began to make pancakes as thin as matzohs. I baked them on the hot plate and strung them like beads on a string over our heads. The circles of baked dough began to rot after a few days. We took them down and dried them again, making them smaller. Finally they were hard like rocks but could not be preserved, even this way, because of the mice. Attracted by the smell of food, they traveled down the string, eating the precious food we tried to store. We could not chase them away. We soon experienced similar disillusionment when we tried to store water. Our dream was to save a full barrel of water but this remained just that, a dream. We were always a drink too short and could never conserve any.

And so 20 months had passed in this way. When we first went underground the hole was cold. Pinek brought us blankets which we hung on the earthen walls for warmth. But these had long since rotted away. In the beginning we remained in our original clothing but it had become increasingly warm so we had taken off the clothing. The men used their clothes for pillows. I hung my dress and shoes above the hotplate.

Even in winter we soon discovered that our hole stayed warm enough from the heat of our bodies. Our clothes rotted in the dampness but my brothers didn't worry about it. They said they'd go out naked if they lived.

We hadn't washed in over a year. One could not imagine that we would have been able to survive this way for so long, but we did. When we first went into hiding we had thought it would only be for a few weeks. But now we were into our second winter and we had become accustomed to our cave life. We felt as though we had grown into that broken cot we had set up in the beginning, as though we had become part of the board beneath us. We were in an earthen box 1.9 meters long and 1.4 meters wide. It was no more than 1.2 meters high at its highest point. We hadn't stood up in all that time. On our knees our heads almost hit the ceiling. We never stretched out our legs because there was no room. Two people could lie north to south, in the center, and two east to west at either end. No one could stretch out his legs. A board, supported by an empty water barrel on one end, the hot plate and some metal scraps on the other, served as our cot. Dad and I lay on this board. Pinek lay on an additional smaller board, close to the opening in the ceiling. We occupied the same individual space for the whole two years of our confinement.

Of course we tried to maximize the frequency with which we changed our positions in this space. We could sit with our legs tucked under us and stand on our knees. But we could not extend our limbs. In all this time, we had not used our legs.

We had one pot, four spoons and four cups for water. These were our only utensils. We didn't need any more. I peeled potatoes in a sitting position and cooked them. There was hardly any air. All we had came in from a crack in the wall leading to the cellar. The cellar, itself, was littered with Józio's scraps and wires and filled with dust and the earth we had dug up.

Into these horrid conditions we now had to add another person, Anna. Pinek, whose position was next to the trap door, pulled her down to us. She remained sitting silently for a while, looking at each of us with eyes filled with tears. No one could find a word to say. I had already prepared the soup. I put the pot in the middle of the cot, which served as our table, and everybody dug in with his spoon. As soon as we started eating the rat came for his portion, appearing in the crack where he had made a tunnel. When Anna saw him she nearly screamed.

Her first reaction to our condition was that she would give herself up to the Gestapo rather than remain in our hiding place for even a single day. She was, of course, foolish to say this because it was not only her own or our lives she threatened but also the lives of all the people who were helping us. We had to suffer and survive together. There was no alternative.

I put my arm around her and stroked her. "You will get used to it ... slowly," I said. Like the rest of us she received a corner on the common cot, a spoon and an earphone for the radio. None of us had or needed more.

Our home, which had been tight for the four of us, now became even more of a trial for us with five. The lack of adequate air and the choking heat were nearly impossible to bear. Our food supply grew smaller every day. The closer the front moved to us the harder it became to obtain any kind of food. Whoever had grain or flour stored it for himself. The little pancakes that I had prepared for the most critical time we would not touch, even after days of fasting. I dried them over and over again in order to keep them in good condition. As long as we still had electric power Józio always managed to get us a few potatoes to cook. It was much worse later, when the electric power was cut off.

We listened now to the movement of the fighting forces on both fronts, one between the Russians and the Germans, the other between the Allies and the Germans. The Russians were making great strikes, chasing the Germans from their territory. There was fighting in the west Ukraine by then and the Polish underground was preparing to join the Russians in chasing the Germans out of their lands. Groups of partisans were in the forests ready for action. The underground held secret meetings. At one meeting they were asked whether they would take Jews into their organization to fight alongside them. The answer was no. Józio was disappointed. Single Jews who had joined the Polish partisans never revealed their identities to them.

I should explain to you here that the Polish underground was divided into two parts. The group that our Józio belonged to was called the Armia Krajowa, the Home Army. They were the right wing of the resistance and were the only group in our area. The

Armia Krajowa's inclination was to support the Western Allies England, France and the United States. They wanted to see a free economy and a democratic political system in Poland after the war. The other resistance group was known as the Armia Ludowa, and they had the opposite political orientation. They leaned to the left and looked to Russia as their model. Their hope was that the end of the war would see the triumph of a socialist democratic government, committed to the interests of workers.

Another difference between the Home Army and the Armia Ludowa was their feelings about Jews. Jews were gladly accepted as resistance fighters into the Communist group, which, in its left wing ideology, accepted Jews into the socialist society of the future. But the Armia Krajowa held the same ideas about Jews as did most of the Polish population: they wanted nothing to do with Jews.

The Allied Front moved slowly and surely but not in the way we had hoped. When one's time is running out, one dreams of quick action and big operations. Whenever we heard the Allies had moved forward only two or three kilometers, we were consumed with disappointment. It meant the enemy was still strong and that the war might still last another year or two. It meant, of course, that we would not see victory. At such times we were unbearably bitter and would certainly have been better off without the radio. We lived in the unknown, far from reality, suspended, waiting, hoping for a miracle.

Better reports came from the Russian Front though. There were breaks in enemy lines here and there at a distance of 15 kilometers from us.

Soon we began to hear the first bombers in our region. We heard that long-awaited sound with mixed feelings, especially when shrapnel tore holes through our living quarters. To us it was the same familiar question: would we live or die?

As we had feared, our electricity was soon cut off and we were plunged into darkness. We were out of food, too. All we had were a few raw potatoes and no way to cook them. After a few days of hunger we tried to eat them but we couldn't. We tried to grate or scrape one of the potatoes. Perhaps it would be edible then, but, even so, we couldn't eat it. It was impossible to swallow even a bite. How spoiled and helpless a human being is and how different from all other creatures, not to be able to maintain himself without cooking! We were now completely dependent on our guardian angel, Józio.

We heard the bombers more often now. We met each air raid with prayer. My heart and thoughts were always, always with you. God would save you, I believed, as He had until now.

We had no more light from that tiny bulb around which our lives had revolved every evening as we huddled together on the broken cot. Daylight and sunshine had become dim memories, tucked far back in our recollections of the past.

We could no longer even supply Józio with news as we had been doing every evening since he had brought the radio to us. We now waited for news from him, hoping it would be good, and he understood how important this now was for us. Our power of resistance was very low. We were ravenously hungry all the time and Józio was practically helpless to alter that. The front was moving closer, the rationing of the food for the population above ground becoming tighter each day. It was nearly impossible for him to take anything unnoticed from his home.

Now we had a bite to eat no more than once every two days, causing us to be weak from hunger and utterly exhausted. The pancakes we had prepared for this time were long gone. They had fed the mice more than us. We had very little water and the insects were all but unbearable as we fought them off in the utter darkness.

One evening Józio mentioned he had some wheat bran. Pinek asked him to bring it and, little by little, only he was able to eat it. None of the rest of us would. We watched him eating and he said, sarcastically, that when the liberation came, he would be the only one left alive if we insisted on not helping ourselves as he did. But I couldn't swallow any of it. There was more straw in it than bran.

At this time we discussed with Józio the possibility of bringing Franka in on our secret. Only if she knew about us and allowed him to bring us a little more food could we hope to keep from starving. Józio was hesitant and very reluctant to do this, not at all certain her reaction would be positive. He believed, probably more than we did, that we could continue to live by miracles alone.

We continued to plead with him to speak to his wife. But our condition, near death as we were, spoke more loudly to him than our words. Józio finally told her, and a true miracle occurred. The mystery about her husband and the other woman now solved, Franka was pacified. But when she realized the implications of her actions, she was horrified, realizing she had endangered her family and all of us.

Though she had little herself, she prepared for us, each evening, a few cooked potatoes. Sometimes she sent a piece of bread and some sour milk. With this food, sent regularly for a few weeks, we slowly began to regain our strength.

Reports from the eastern front were daily more encouraging; we anxiously awaited liberation. But suddenly, after liberating Przemysl, Dynow, Brzozow and Sanok, the Russian march turned westward, leaving Lesko, with us in it, still in the hands of the Germans.

In the last days before liberation, the Germans were demonic. They searched houses and cellars, looking for ammunition, radios, machinery, whatever might be hidden and used against them. People were accused of sabotage and murdered. The Germans robbed and plundered wherever they could. One day they came to Józio's workshop and then down into the cellar looking for machinery. They noticed a wet spot on the floor and asked Józio what he had hidden there. They didn't believe his denials and began digging, not two meters from where we were hidden.

They worked for two hours, coming ever closer to us. The tension in our hole was indescribable. We were so close to being discovered when we heard them suddenly throw down their shovels with the words "zum Teufel" (to the devil) and left.

It was August 2, 1944 when we heard machine gun fire for the first time. We listened attentively to the shooting which lasted all day, thinking the labor pains of liberation had begun. How can I tell you our feelings then, our excitement? Józio did not show up at the workshop all that day and we prayed nothing had happened to him.

That evening we heard the door open roughly and two men speaking Russian walked in. It was the first patrol in town. They searched the house. We listened anxiously, full of expectation. It's a good thing we didn't let Milek shout a greeting to our liberators as he wanted to do. We might have been shot before we had time to explain who and what we were.

They left and hours passed though Józio didn't return. "Why doesn't he come to announce the happy moment for which we've been waiting so long?," we asked ourselves, puzzled.

At noon on the following day, Milek, not being able to wait any longer, pushed the board above our heads up. He wanted to get into the kitchen, look out the window and see what was happening. At that very moment, Józio arrived. When he saw Milek he shoved him back into the hole explaining that the Russians we had heard were only a guerilla patrol and that the Germans were back in town. The Germans were in retreat from the East and were now stuck in Lesko. Those Germans who had fled on August 2nd had destroyed the two bridges on the San River as they retreated. Now the seventh Panzer division was in Lesko, stranded, trying to repair the bridges as quickly as possible while the Russians kept them under constant fire. We were in the middle of the fighting zone although sitting tightly underground.

Our hole was now breaking apart. Pieces of the wall were caving in. It wasn't long before a bomb fell on a machine that was sitting in Józio's kitchen. It was a miracle it didn't destroy the kitchen floor altogether. Our hole had become too dangerous to live in any longer and we renewed our efforts to persuade Józio to move us to the house where his family lived.

Józio's cow helped us reach a decision. It became sick and needed immediate care. Józio couldn't afford to lose it. Pinek and Milek were both expert in handling sick cattle and Józio pulled them out of the hole to help him. They stretched their muscles for a long time before they were able to stand. Their legs which had not walked for nearly two years refused to function.

Then they had to walk to Józio's house one hundred meters away, under cover of darkness. After much pain and struggling with their muscles, they arrived at the barn which was behind the house. They worked on the cow all night and in the morning went into Józio's house and remained there all day. The cow improved.

The cellar in Józio's house was filled with stacks of firewood. He made room amid the firewood for a new hideout. Our hole was almost demolished by this time, riddled by shrapnel and bullet holes. When the new place was ready we made the decision to move to the house.

That evening we were ready to go. I took down my surviving dress and shoes which I had cared for all this time. They were still in good condition. I had hoped for so long that this day would come and now at last it had. I put on my dress and pulled the shoes over my swollen feet, but I couldn't tie the strings.

We had no bundles or luggage of any kind; nothing to carry but ourselves. It was the easiest move we ever made in one sense, Rena, but the hardest in many ways, too.

We crawled out of the hole, blinded by the evening darkness, Daddy almost naked. We stretched our painful muscles, our thoughts concentrating on only one thing: the one hundred meters we would have to walk, unseen, to Józio's door. Our legs were so swollen we could hardly stand.

We decided to make the move in two phases. Your father went out first, alone, and Józio, Anna and I followed after. It's hard to describe what a strange feeling it was to walk on our legs again. They didn't feel like legs at all after all the time that had passed. When your father reached the threshold of Józio's door, he was so weak he couldn't lift his leg to make the final step. Unable to move any other way, he fell face forward over the threshold and had to be dragged, pushed and pulled inside by Józio's sixteen-year-old daughter.

Franka greeted us with a kind smile. The smaller children were asleep, the older ones silent. No one spoke, as if nothing unusual was occurring.

Franka gave us a warm supper and then we went down to the cellar. Our little area was concealed by walls of firewood, but it wasn't very safe. In fact, it was a most dangerous time, with Germans retreating and the Russians only about a kilometer away. The Germans were by now both bloodthirsty and reckless and everyone feared what would come next.

Józio's family was terribly hungry and we were now a part of their little world. They shared whatever they had with us but, in truth, they had practically nothing. Under a rain of bullets in the middle of a bombing, dear Franka dug potatoes from a nearby field to feed her hungry family. That evening I came upstairs and helped her as much as I could in the house. Little Lusia was a year old and I found her crying, in need of attention, and so I took over caring for her.

We made soup from potatoes. A pinch of flour was roasted on the stove for flavoring. The hungry children gobbled it up from the pan, still uncooked. Staszek came to help us, having already been released from jail. He went off, hunting for food, and hired himself out to work for peasants in the countryside. A week later he brought back a half sack of grain. We ground a little of it each day in order to conserve it.

My brothers spent their time chopping wood in the cellar while Anna and I helped out with the household chores in the evenings.

The children were marvelous. They didn't speak a word about us to any of the neighbors and we thanked God every minute that we were alive.

The shooting and bombings increased daily and the frightened children gathered around their mother, praying out loud. A bomb fell into the house at one point, tearing off the front wing. But no one was hurt.

Each time the shooting stopped, Józio ran out to see what was going on. Several people had been killed or injured by the constant bombs.

We had now been in Józio's house for about three weeks. When we first came up out of the hole, the dark cellar, with its tiny covered window, had seemed so bright we could hardly stand it. Our eyes, not having seen daylight for almost two years couldn't even bear that dim light. Coming up from the staircase of the cellar into the hall, the sparkle of twilight which we could see through a crack in the wall was so bright it almost blinded us. I wondered how people could bear to walk in the sunlight in the middle of the day. According to your father, it was miraculous we had not been blinded or crippled after those two years in the hole. Milek, who had once said he didn't want to live, now said it wouldn't have mattered to him if he were blind or crippled. He only wanted to feel the warmth of the sun on his body once more. That was all he wanted out of life, that and two goats for milk and to stretch out in the grass under the warm sun again. Such were our dreams for the future but even at that point, with our liberation so near, our mental and physical exhaustion was so severe that we feared we would not live to see it.

Suddenly we got shocking news. The whole region was to be evacuated. Every living soul, big and small, was to retreat with the Germans. We were struck dumb. What were we to do now? We couldn't mix with the population, we'd be recognized instantly. We were yellow and looked like the lime we had been living in while the general population was brown from the sun. We couldn't remain behind because that would be certain death. The villages around Lesko had already been evacuated. Not a soul had been left.

We didn't know what had happened to you. The latest report was that Magda, you and Stasia had moved away. But we didn't know where. Janek was arrested by the Gestapo on the night before evacuation was to begin at 4:00 AM on the 14th of September, 1944. We had to reach a decision quickly but Milek was almost paralyzed with pain from sciatica while Anna had developed acute appendicitis. It was a night of fear and despair.

Józio was with us and we discussed what to do. We lacked medications and had no transportation. It was impossible for us to go anywhere. We thought of Dr. Lisikiewicz, who had refused to help us at the start of our stay in the hole under the cellar floor. We had long suspected that he had hidden his Jewish nurse, Irena. At last we determined that we had no choice but to send Józio to him and gave Józio a list of the medications we needed.

He came to Dr. Lisikiewicz and said, "Please don't ask any questions. Give me these medications because they are urgently needed." He gave him what he asked for.

With God's help and your father's constant attention, the pain subsided for both Milek and Anna and we prepared ourselves to move.

We washed and combed our hair. The men shaved. At dawn we would be ready to leave the house. Of course we would be walking at a great distance from Józio and his family.

No one slept that night. At 2 A.M., Józio went outside and saw no Germans. We could hear the noises of heavy traffic moving away from us along the road.

The town was silent, still asleep. There was an expectation of something new, something wonderful on the still air.

It was a peaceful morning. No shooting. Franka made everyone coffee and we drank it in silent expectation. Our heads were dizzy with happy and unhappy thoughts, with curiosity and anxiety. I hoped you were well and Janek alive. I thought of so many things and suddenly I found that I couldn't keep my eyes open. I wanted to lose myself in my thoughts for a while and I fell asleep.

I was awakened by the loud voice and happy face of Józio, standing in the doorway of the cellar. "We're free, free," he was saying, "The Russians are here! We're free."

The superhuman strength that had kept us alive all these past months and years failed us now. We remained motionless. Only tears, like a quiet stream, flowed down our cheeks. Józio's words echoed over and over in my ears. I whispered the traditional prayer: "Blessed art Thou, O Lord our God, King of the Universe, who has sustained us to this day!"

I can't remember now whether it was a feeling of happiness, of utter exhaustion or just one of complete sorrow that overcame me. The words of Polish poet Juluis Slowacki, recalling the lament of a Bedouin nomad over the loss of his family from plague in the desert, came to my mind.

"O! Gorzka wolnosc i chwila odlotu!
Jam do ciemnego juz przywykl namiotu."
"Oh bitter freedom and moment of flight,
I am already accustomed to the dark sight."

All these years we had been praying for just this moment. And now we were numb.

After a long while we were able to move. We went out of the cellar and kissed the people who had been our saviors all these long, dark months. Slowly, ever so slowly, a new excitement overwhelmed us.

I looked out the window. A little park surrounding Józio's house was full of Russian soldiers, cleaning their horses. Heavy war machinery stood in the streets. The faces of the soldiers seemed as tired as our own. They cleaned and dusted and washed themselves as best they could in the park. What a wonderful sight!

We decided to leave Lesko immediately, not wanting to remain in the middle of the front lines of the fighting. We looked at one another, our faces swollen and discolored, our legs bloated and so heavy we could hardly stand on them. How would we walk the 15 kilometers to Sanok?

Józio thought this a very bad idea and tried to dissuade us, but our desire to try was stronger than our physical weakness.

We were still afraid to have it revealed that we had survived, but Józio laughed at our fears and insisted that everyone should know. And so we soon had visitors, the first of whom was Dr. Lisikiewicz, as glad to see us alive as we were to see him. He had saved three Jewish women: his nurse, Irena, and two of the Steinmetz sisters. We finally understood his actions.

Then Józio went to see Stefan, Janek's brother, and learned from him that you, too, were well and that all of you were back in the forest again. If anything could have given us the strength to make the trip before us, it was that piece of news.

At eleven in the morning of September 15, 1944, we left Józio's house, hobbling weakly on canes but strong in our resolution. We tottered through the town in which 5,000 Jews had once lived. We were all that remained alive of these, we and two others, Bronka Schwartz and Franek Hirsch. The three women Dr. Lisikiewicz had saved were not originally from Lesko.

We could not have imagined that life could proceed normally in Lesko, not as it had before the war, with such a large part of its population obliterated. But the sun was shining, people were bustling about busily. Grocers, shoemakers, dressmakers, watch repair shops ... all were open. All these had been Jewish occupations in Poland.

People were out in the streets. Curious children crowded around soldiers and stared at their now unfamiliar uniforms and equipment.

It was so strange, this walk of ours through a familiar town that now looked like another planet. Everybody on the street looked at us as though we were the strangers from Mars. It's true we did look a little strange and our existence was a mystery to those who saw us. The expressions on the faces of those we passed seemed to be saying, "What are you doing among the living?"

People we had known before the war now looked at us with such an expression of indifference that we were taken aback. What had happened to them to make them so unfeeling? How could it be that none of them asked what had happened to us? That none offered us their help? Not even the slightest degree of concern could we see in their faces.

Keeping our eyes on the road ahead, saying nothing to anyone, we left the town. The road was filled with Russian military vehicles and artillery. On one massive gun sat a husky Russian girl, about nineteen or twenty, with a grenade in each hand. No one paid any attention to our slow progress in the ditch along the side of the road.

We walked a little and then rested. The fresh, clean fall air, which we took in by the lungful for the first time in twenty-two months made us drowsy. We lay down on the grass to enjoy the warm sun. It was a beautiful day. Everything around us was so lovely—the grass, the many colors of the trees, the cool shadows and peaceful forest. We couldn't rest long because the sun was beginning to set and we knew we had to reach a community before nightfall. We pulled our shoes back on our swollen feet, picked up our canes, and continued walking.

It was already very dark when we reached the outskirts of Zagorz. We couldn't go any farther and stopped at a bakery in the town. Two young workers were about to close the store but they saw how tired we were and asked us to sit down. Without any other questions they brought us fresh coffee and bread, still hot from the oven. It was wonderful.

We told the young men where we were heading and asked to be allowed to sleep at the bakery for the night. They brought us a few empty sacks to place on the stone floor, locked us in the shop and left.

With great effort we pulled off our shoes and lay down. This was our first night of freedom, what we had longed for and dreamed of for so long. We savored every moment though our bodies ached. My thoughts were all with you and I wished I were a bird to fly off and find you. How lucky we were to have survived and know you had, too. Wrapped in these thoughts, I felt as though I were on a soft bed and slept deeply.

We were awake in the early morning, before the bakery opened. Soon an elderly man and one of the boys from the night before entered. The man was not unfriendly but very quiet and, after we exchanged greetings with him, we prepared to leave. But we could hardly lift ourselves up from the floor. Our legs, which had been unused for so long, simply refused to carry us farther. The muscles had atrophied from disuse and malnutrition and would not work. Still, we forced ourselves up and, leaning heavily on our canes, hobbled to the road. There were still eight kilometers ahead of us to Sanok.

The fresh fall air was exhilarating despite our severely weakened condition. On the road the army was steadily moving westward. We allowed ourselves some time to sit by the side of the road and rest. Suddenly, a wagon pulled by a pair of large, brown horses, stopped in front of us. A Russian officer told his soldiers who were riding in it to step down and help us up into the wagon. This officer, a captain, had a long mustache and a friendly manner. The soldiers asked him if he knew us. Of course, he said to them, they are Jews. He told them to give us food, and they did.

On the road to Sanok he spoke to us, telling us he was also a Jew. The long mustache he wore was to fool the Germans if he were captured. He pulled a small prayer book out of his pocket. "During the three years I have been at the front with the artillery," he told us, "I've never failed to pray."

It seemed strange to us for a young Russian, raised under Communism, to have such sentiments.

We ate the bread and salami they gave us in silence, only a deep sigh from one or the other of us breaking through now and then. This Russian asked us no question; it seemed he already knew the answers.

Soon we found ourselves in Sanok. The Russian let us down in the center of the town. There we said goodbye. Sanok had been free for six weeks, and there were a few survivors there. We greeted each other as though we were from a single family. We gathered in Dr. Lerner's room in his father's house, talking and crying. We all had so much to tell one another ... and so many questions. There was no end to the questions.

When evening approached we realized we had nowhere to sleep. But we weren't worried. There were many empty houses around us. We chose one and entered it. There was no glass in any of the windows but we lay down there, anyway, on the bare floor and rested for the night.

The next day one of your father's former patients brought us some kitchen utensils and then we began to dust and clean the place. A new life was beginning for us.

We decided to borrow several beds, some blankets and some pillows.

Your father visited his friend and colleague, Dr. N. He was a middle-aged man with a wife, well established in the town. Daddy was sure he would help us during these initial, critical weeks. But when Dr. N. saw your father, he received him coldly, like a stranger. He offered no words of sympathy or even gladness at seeing him alive. Daddy felt a lump in his throat and decided not to say why he had come.

Dr. N. complained bitterly about how he had been ruined by the war. When your father left, he gave him one blanket and a pillow—on "loan" and only for a short time. "Until you can buy your own," he said. After three weeks, he sent his servant to retrieve them.

After such a reception at the home of a "friend," we did not try to get help anywhere else. We heard from our neighbors that some people in town had great collections of furnishings from Jewish homes. We thought we might get some things from them to fix up the house in which we found ourselves so we could bring our child home. This desire, in fact, was stronger than everything else. Now that we were free, every minute that kept us apart from you seemed like a year.

Food, of course, was an urgent need. People looked at us with great curiosity but no one asked whether we were hungry, no one offered us help. Not showing interest in us under such circumstances as these was unfathomable. One couldn't help but wonder about the mystery of human nature at such times. It was so terribly sad to feel so unwanted. I pitied those people, who were so filled with hatred and selfishness.

We had some pots but nothing to cook in them. On the outskirts of town, a few kilometers away, there were some vegetables on what had formerly been Jewish fields. We received the new owner's permission to collect them and to dig for potatoes. Two or three times a week we left in the morning and returned in the evening with bags of vegetables that we shared with other unfortunates.

As the front moved westward, other Jews were liberated and they all gathered in Sanok. Our "family"' grew greater each day. Over the next few weeks the number of returning Jews reached its maximum: eighty persons ... all that remained from the original 30,000 Jews in the region before the war.

Each of these eighty survivors was alone, tired, broken, both physically and mentally. It was difficult for any of them to even begin to contemplate starting a new life. Each needed immediate and extensive help.

The Russian Jews in the army contributed considerably while they were stationed in town. Russian Jews, though, were known for their coldness. They had little interest in their heritage and mixed marriages were common in Russia. But when the Nazis reached deep into their country, too, how bitterly were they disappointed! The slaughter of Jewish families by the population reminded one of the old Tzarist antisemitism, a bit of the worst side of human nature sneaking out from behind the revolutionary code.

However, the Jewish officers of the Russian army that we met were warm and human. They spoke movingly of their long marches through cities and towns, all through western Ukraine, without meeting a single Jew. They helped us furnish a little home where we could bring our child. They secured some food and medicines for us, too, trying their best to make our recovery possible.

Your father was on crutches for over three months. Milek has terrible sciatica to this day. Pinek was terribly broken and suffers nightmares even now. Of all the family, I was the strongest and, after six weeks, I decided to bring you home. I got a lift to Lesko and visited Józio and his family there.

I was too excited to rest long in Józio's house and went immediately to see Stefan, Janek's brother. He was surprised to see me but I was so happy to see him and his family. Stefan offered to walk with me through the forest and all the way there he kept trying to prepare me for the difficulty 1 might have in taking you away with me. Too much time had elapsed. You were used to a different way of life now, he said. I told him I would give you freedom to choose for the time being and that I hoped we could win back your love and your confidence in us.

We walked slowly, he easing his pace to suit mine. My feet ached and my steps were weak but I felt like I was flying. I was very excited. I tried to imagine how you looked now, how you had grown in those two years.

We were close to the little clearing. I looked up and there you were in the yard with Magda. You turned and looked at me with surprise in your beautiful eyes. I stretched out my arms to you and you ran into them. "My mother, my mother," you kept repeating.

I was so happy and so tired I couldn't bear it.

You clung to me from that moment and did not let me out of your sight. That night we both slept in one bed, but neither of us really slept. We were both so happy, so excited. You couldn't wait till morning when we were to go to Sanok to see your father.

In the morning Magda prepared breakfast for all and Janek snapped a few pictures of us. Then we were ready to part. I felt so humble and filled with gratitude. I couldn't find the words to express myself. How does one thank another for saving one's child?

Janek remained in the doorway of the little hut as we departed, watching us walk down the road, out of sight, with shifting emotions flying across his face. He had become very attached to you, and I guessed how he must have felt at that moment.

All the way to Sanok you asked anxiously, "Where is my home?" and "Where is my Daddy?"

Your father came running to you when we came, at last, to Sanok, followed by Pinek, Milek and Anna. And then all the survivors were around you. It was such a joyous, such a special reunion.

At the time we had with us an elderly cousin who had also survived. We called him "grandpa" and he became your grandpa, especially, because you could not remember your own.

To everyone in our little family you became "our child." The survivors loved you and cared for you because you were the only surviving Jewish child in our region. You were precious to us all.

A different life now began for us. You woke up early in the morning, as you had in the forest. Grandpa gave you breakfast, allowing the rest of us to sleep a little longer. But we didn't really sleep. We listened to your conversation and to your laughter. Life began, slowly, to normalize and we began to worry about the little things, about this and that, the necessities of daily living.

Józio visited us and brought us a little money that we had given him and he had saved for us. He also brought a gold watch and gave it to us, saying "You must have something to start with and I don't need it."

If there were more human beings like Józio in the world ... ah, what a world it would be.

In one of the rooms of the house we readied a little office for Daddy. Dr. Lisikiewicz lent him a stethoscope and a few other instruments to enable him to examine patients.

The news of our survival spread quickly, and some peasants came to the office. They brought food and household goods— more valuable to us than money—as payment.

Your uncles kidded each other about marriage and Pinek said he would marry the first woman that came back to Sanok. When Pepka Mund, known to us as Marisia, came to town to search for family, she found herself a husband! She had survived all this time with Aryan papers.

We prepared a memorable wedding, almost like old times. I cooked and baked with the help of Estka and Dora Amster in their apartment. All of the eighty Jews were present and grandpa performed the wedding ceremony. The first and best man at the groom's side of course was Józio, who gave the couple his blessings.

Ela came to Sanok too. She learned that her two sisters had been saved by Dr. Lisikiewicz. She was the one for whom the Aryan papers were intended and to whom I had given them —resisting the temptation to keep them for myself. We became friends.

She hugged you with tears in her eyes. She had had a daughter your age who she couldn't save. She had given the child to a Christian family along with all of her possessions. After she had gone, the family surrendered the child to the Gestapo. All the years Ela lived as a Christian she had believed her child was alive. Only after the liberation did she discover the truth, and now the three sisters clung together with the joy of finding one another again and with the sorrow of what they had lost.

## CHAPTER SEVEN

# LAND OF THE FREE

We did not enjoy freedom for very long, however. After three months there were fresh victims among the survivors. Some had tried to enter former property and were killed by their former neighbors. Others were killed, not because they tried to reclaim their lost homes but because their neighbors were afraid they would. The air again became hard to breathe. Fear returned to us and we began to dream of escape. But to where? And how? We had no strength to travel and no means of transportation.

Soon the Nazis were completely defeated and the concentration camps were opened. The Russians guarding our borders allowed some wandering survivors into the territory to look for family and a place of safety, where they could feel accepted. From these people we learned of an existing Jewish community in Bucharest and, more important, of a ship waiting in Constanta to take Jews to Palestine. That ship became our hope and our destination.

Your uncles and aunts were reluctant to leave immediately. Such a trip would be a very big undertaking. But we knew we were all risking our lives by remaining in Poland.

Three weeks passed before we made our decision. We decided that first you, me and Daddy would leave and your uncles and

Anna would follow at the next opportunity. Pinek became sick for a week after we had made the decision to go.

Our friend Ela decided to come with us and leave her sisters behind. She had received information that her husband was alive in Rumania and she wanted to join him.

It was March 15, 1945, a Saturday night. A Czech army officer in town for a few days had slept in our house that night. He offered to take us to the Czech border in his car.

The next morning, when we were ready to leave, there was a blinding snowstorm and a freezing wind. The family begged us not to go, to postpone the trip, but we were determined to leave that morning. We did, but with heavy hearts.

The car barely moved. Finally we arrived in Krosno, a town on the road to the Czech border. The snow reached our thighs and we could go no farther. We found a place to sleep as the weather worsened. All transportation had stopped and we were told it might take weeks to repair the train. We were all sick. It seemed senseless to remain any longer, waiting, and so, at the first opportunity, we returned to Sanok. But while in Krosno we had learned of an organization which helped people cross the border. We knew the right people to approach but we had to wait for better weather.

On March 23, 1945 we left Sanok again, this time for good. We reached Munkachewo, Czechoslovakia on a Russian truck. From there we hitchhiked and walked for days until we finally reached Bucharest. I recall the comical and often sad incidents along the way when we had to pretend we belonged to various nationalities, speak many languages, to get across the various borders and checkpoints.

You, my dear, spoke only Polish. In Satmara, Rumania, we were asked why you spoke a different language from us. We were afraid of Russian spies, afraid we might be forced to return to Poland, and told them you were a relative we were caring for.

We told one man, in whose house we were staying, that you were our Polish niece. He flushed with excitement and then began to sob. "Give me this child and she will be my daughter. I lost my whole family. I was a very wealthy man and I will still get my property back. You are going into the unknown. Let me take care of her, at least until you settle somewhere." Instead of an answer, I cried with him.

In Bucharest we rented a room from a nice couple in a country house on the outskirts of the city. Do you remember the friendly landlady, Mrs. Jorgescu? You used to climb in her cherry trees.

Ela stayed with us while trying to locate her husband. She had the address of people he had lived with, but when she went there she found he had moved away. She learned that he had already gone to Palestine, which was our goal as well.

We soon met refugees from all over Europe. They were the surviving inmates of the recently liberated concentration camps and those who, like us, had been in hiding. We met in the Joint Distribution Committee Building in Bucharest where we had all gone for help. The scene there was truly tragic. The people there looked like walking skeletons in striped costumes. Some women had shaved heads. The grounds were filthy. Human feces littered the yard. The stench and flies were everywhere. The hopelessness and despondency of the people was inescapable. They sat or milled about aimlessly ...waiting.

One saw heartbreaking scenes there daily. A father and daughter had sat on a bench, next to each other, not recognizing one another until they began to talk. Sister and brother, husband and wife ... all were unrecognizable to one another, even after a short parting.

There was no place to put these people; nowhere to send them. The Jewish community of Bucharest, what was left of it, joined in the work of rehabilitation, caring for some of the refugees. The hospitals in the city were filled to overflowing.

The only hope and destination for all these people was Palestine. The Zionist committee promised them passage. No one knew when, however. Everyone had been registered to go - and now they were waiting, simply waiting.

Luckily it was an early spring that year in Bucharest in 1945. Surrounding the building in which we found ourselves was a garden. Refugees could rest and heal their sores in the sun there while waiting for news of their promised emigration. But soon the Russian NKVD began snooping around that gathering.

They now called on everyone to register for repatriation. We all remembered the "repatriation" registrations of 1940, when instead of going home, tens of thousands of people wound up in Siberia. Besides, none of us wanted to go back to Poland or any other country in Europe only to face new pogroms. No matter what we had already suffered, everyone of us was determined to surmount every obstacle to reach the Holy Land.

The Zionist organization registered relatives of the Jews in Palestine first. Ela was among the first in this happy, preferential quota. We had been together in Bucharest three months when we finally parted. Like many others, we left for Hungary to avoid the registration for repatriation.

The watchman at the station and other officials were paid to take our whole group to Hungary, and we waited long hours for the freight train that would take us there. We were happy to be leaving Bucharest. The train finally arrived and we boarded and found places to sit. It was very quiet, exhausted passengers resting and listening to the monotonous rumble of the rail cars - a sound that, unfortunately, reminded us of the past but which we now hoped would take us closer to a happier future.

Suddenly harsh, commanding voices broke the stillness. Russian soldiers, jumping from train car to train car shouted "Jews, give up your possessions!" Anxiety appeared on the faces before me. Imagine what possessions these soldiers could find there. We tried explaining that these people had barely escaped with their lives and had nothing of value left, but it was in vain. They fired shots into the air to scare us. Some people who tried to protect what little property they still had were beaten up. You, dear Rena, were so scared that you begged everyone to give the soldiers everything so that we could remain alive. After they had robbed us, the soldiers left. And we, all of us, after this, got off at the next station. There at least it was light and we could wait through the night and board another train in the morning. We sat on our bundles on the train platform as armed guards circulated among the passengers. Suddenly you, Rena, jumped off the platform and began to run across the tracks, ducking under stationary trains, across dark rails until you fell and cut your hand on the sharp stones of the train bed. Your father ran after you and grabbed you up from the darkness before the train that was then approaching reached you.

I cannot forget that night. We sat on the platform of that small station, on the way to Hungary. The night was clear and chilly. We didn't sleep but watched the sky and saw the dawn break in rosy rays of light that soothed us, like balm to our shattered spirits.

A train arrived in the morning and took us straight to Budapest. We slept there only one night and left promptly for Gratz, Austria the following day. Our group stayed close together as we traveled from country to country aiming always toward Palestine.

After two days in Gratz, we came closer to the border, to a small village occupied by the British who kept us in a camp. There, for the first time, we met Jewish soldiers from Palestine who had fought with the British in the war. They were known as the Jewish Brigade and they greeted us with open arms, taking us into their hearts. It was from them that we discovered, with great disappointment, that England had taken a negative position on our immigration to Palestine.

This was heartwrenching news. After all we had been through, all the pain, the suffering, were we to be denied this, too? We were shattered and didn't know where to turn. In addition, not one of us had any identification; no birth certificates, no marriage licenses, no documents of any kind, only the numbers the Germans had tattooed on our arms. Where could we go?

An official of the Jewish Brigade came to lift our spirits and promised we would go to the Holy Land, with or without permission. We had to get out of the transit camp, but the English wouldn't let us go any farther. After a week we received secret notice to leave our luggage behind and to go, singly or in couples, for a walk in the forest. Late in the afternoon, on a lovely spring day, we all took that walk. One after another we emptied the camp and met again in the woods where trucks were waiting for us. We crossed the Italian border in these and passed through a beautiful valley beneath the Alps. We were housed in temporary shelters and our possessions brought to us the next day.

From Treviso, where we were first brought and cared for by the Jewish soldiers, we were taken to Modena, also in northern Italy. We were put into a British transit camp there, together with other foreigners. Here we stayed two weeks and were treated, more or less, like prisoners. Conditions were poor—inadequate hygiene, overcrowding—but we weren't permitted to leave. Single people left illegally, to seek their fortunes on their own, but it became impossible for our group to continue its journey.

One lucky day we obtained a ride from an automobile driver on his way to Rome. We were glad to go with him. Your father had saved his medical diploma and he immediately took it to the Allied Commission when we arrived, seeking an appointment as a physician somewhere in Italy. One had to make a living, even while waiting to emigrate. He was given a job immediately in a Polish-English camp for army families and we were delighted with our good fortune. We needed the work and, even more, a home and peace.

The camp was in Barletta, a town in the southern hills of the Italian peninsula. The journey itself was actually pleasant, until we began to experience the heat that was so much a part of that area in Italy. It was our first time in a near tropical climate, though we soon adjusted to it and even began to enjoy it somewhat.

Barletta was a small town, near Bari, a port city. There a unit of the 2nd Polish Corps, part of the British 8th Army, was stationed. We walked into an old building in Barletta and were greeted by a surprised Polish officer who, after reading your father's letter of recommendation, took him directly to the doctor in charge. Dr. G. was a short, energetic man who seemed pleased at our arrival. He assigned your father to the job of organizing a clinic and caring for some 200 children, their teachers, principal and the workers in the dormitory. He also assigned a nurse to assist him.

We occupied a large room next to the clinic and your father began working immediately. All equipment and medicines were brought from the camp one mile away.

The dormitory, school and chapels were housed in a big Gothic-looking stone building, complete with gargoyles. The hot Barletta sun cast dark blue shadows on the deep set window ledges and sculptured facades. You were happy and excited about the prospect of so many other girls to play with. But they were all older than you except for one little girl, the daughter of one of the teachers, little Halina.

The first evening of our arrival we gathered in the dining room for dinner and met the whole group. We weren't warmly received, but we paid little attention to that, thinking we only needed to become acquainted with these people. We were just too tired to be concerned.

Your father began his work examining and vaccinating everyone and seeing to their complaints. Then he organized the infirmary and prepared to give lectures and call meetings, employing the Russian method of group care.

School began and classes met. You sat happily in your class. At seven years old it was all new to you. You had never been to school. I was given a job, too, and became a nurse in the emergency room of the camp, working from eight in the morning to noon each day.

I liked the work and the people I was working with. My afternoons were free, so I had time for many other things. I visited the green market daily and bought fresh fruit and vegetables. Toward the end of each day, we'd all go bathing in the Adriatic Sea and rest on the beach afterwards. It all felt so good and I began thinking this was an ideal place for recovery. We were isolated from the rest of the Polish community there, but we had each other and didn't feel the isolation that much.

But, before long, incidents of an unpleasant nature began occurring. As the only Jewish child in the school, you weren't seated with the other children at meals but had to eat alone at a separate table. You didn't tell us about this until you began to be ostracized in this fashion in the classrooms, the social hall and at play as well. The director of the school, a German sympathizer, spoke openly of her role in assisting in the extermination of Jewish children. When we learned of this, we brought it to the attention of camp officials and they promised to reprimand her. But her behavior only worsened. She spoke about our family, spreading rumors about us and ill will. She accused your father of making sexual advances to the young women of the camp during physical examinations and the situation became very ugly. Fortunately, one of the nurses working with your father came to his defense, saying that she had been at his side during all the examinations and that no improprieties had occurred. We were grateful to her.

Nevertheless, your father was compelled to resign his position and, after a year in Barletta, we returned to Rome. That was in May 1946.

In Rome we resumed contact with the Jewish Relief again. At that time there were two agencies handling the problem of Jewish refugees: the United Nations Relief and Rehabilitation Administration (UNRRA), which concerned itself with the whole scope of the refugee problem after the war, and the Joint Distribution Committee, the American Jewish organization that was specifically concerned with the situation of Jewish refugees.

The Joint Committee knew the details of illegal Jewish emigration to Palestine and unofficially endorsed and assisted this emigration. Officially the organization did no more than provide relief services to the refugees. When your father was hired by the Joint Committee, upon our return to Rome, and given the position of chief doctor responsible for the care of all the refugees in the region outside Rome, he knew his task would be two-fold: 1) to see that the population was in good health and that people with medical problems received proper care and attention, and 2) to examine those people who were waiting to emigrate to Palestine to determine whether they were in good enough condition to face the rugged passage and the life immediately ahead of them.

Among the people your father met in the course of his work were many Jews who had been sent to Siberia by the Russians after the registration of the Polish refugees.

They told of the hardships they had endured in Siberia and the difficulties they had faced in returning from its frigid wastes. Two old friends of ours were part of this group: old Mrs. Orenstein and her son who had studied in the gymnasium with your father. They lived outside the city with a group of Jews who practiced, in a rudimentary way, the principles of collective life that served as the basis for the *kibbutzim* in Palestine.

Your father discovered that Mrs. Orenstein had a heart condition and would not give his permission for her to emigrate. But having survived the war, she was determined not to let his diagnosis stand in her way. We learned later that she and her son set off illegally for Palestine on a ship that was torpedoed by the British and that they were taken to the island of Cyprus. Much later we received a letter from her from the Holy Land.

At this time, the illegal *Aliyah* (emigration to Palestine) movement was at its height. People who were tired of waiting despondently in Displaced Persons camps found every means possible to go to sea. They hired fishing boats—old ones, small ones—and larger war vessels and set out over the Mediterranean waters with as much secrecy as possible.

Your father worked nights examining many who hoped they would be strong enough to board a ship to Palestine. We, too, had hoped to go on one of those ships, but children were not being taken on board and so we remained in Rome. We didn't want to part from you again.

So we turned our thoughts to the United States instead. While we waited in Rome, we hoped to receive mail from my sister, Clarisse, who had immigrated to America with her husband Samuel just before Mussolini came to power in Italy. Our lives in Rome were relatively easy and it wasn't hard to wait at that point. Your father had a regular salary from the Joint Committee and UNRRA. Compared to the Italians in the city, we lived well. And since your father met hundreds of people whom he had known in Poland in the camps surrounding Rome, we had no shortage of people to talk to. At this time even acquaintances greeted one another as brothers. We had all lost so much, so many loved ones, that we valued whoever had survived as though they were family.

It was while we were in Rome that we first heard from my family in Poland and from Józio. In this way we learned that my sister Hela and her husband were alive, too, having been saved by a loyal and wonderful friend. Though this gave us great happiness, the news Józio sent was sadder. Before we left Poland we had warned him not to reveal what he had done for us for fear of his being ostracized by others in his community. But he hadn't listened. "Let them be ashamed they did nothing," he told us.

But when the elders of the town learned that Józio had saved Jews from the Nazis, they reproached him bitterly and organized a boycott of his workshop. No one came into his shop for repairs any longer, he wrote, even though he was the only mechanic in the town. What little work came his way was "under the table" and not adequately paid for. He and his family were now isolated and starving.

We were very distressed to hear this, even though he wrote that if he were ever faced with such a choice again, "I would do no differently."

And so, the end of my story, Rena. There is only this: to tell you how our journey finished. One of the letters we had written while we were waiting in Rome for some chance to go to the United States brought it about. It was a letter we had sent in hope, but also in desperation, to the Police Department in Chicago, Illinois, asking if they could help us discover the whereabouts of one of our cousins, Clara Eckerling. All we knew was that Clara had lived in Chicago before the war and that she was married to a man named Joe. After seven months we heard back. Do you understand how strange this was for us? As far as we were concerned, the United States was another world entirely. To think that someone there would take the time and have the courtesy to respond to our request for help seemed impossible. But the letter came and, with it, an address for Clara and Joe.

We knew the Eckerlings had knowledge of our existence through the Joint Committee. Part of its work was to send information about Jewish survivors who registered there to various headquarters in the United States. And, as it happened, the head of the Joint Committee in Chicago was also the head of the synagogue that Clara and Joe belonged to. Not long after we left Bucharest, where we had registered with the Joint committee, a check for $100 arrived for us there. Though we were already gone, some of the people in Bucharest at this time and whom we met later in the camps outside Rome, told us the money had been sent from Chicago and so we realized that we had been found ... if only to be lost again for a while.

Once we made contact with the Eckerlings our passage was relatively easy. To circumvent the problem of immigration quotas, the Eckerlings obtained illegal immigration papers for your father, stating that he was a rabbi who had been hired by a congregation in America. Though immigration was strictly limited at this time, religious personnel were allowed to enter America freely. In this way we were able to obtain visas when no one else could and, once again, we were among the fortunate few.

We left Italy at last on the 11th of May 1947, traveling to the land of the free on an Italian military vessel called the Saturnia.

Eleven days later we arrived in New York Harbor.

# AFTERWORD

## by Rena Bernstein

On the day before the transfer of the Jews from Lesko to the Zaslaw Concentration Camp, an unknown woman came to our house and took me away. My parents, Natan and Jafa Wallach, stood aside as this stranger grabbed me and carried me, crying and fighting, into the street. My parents stood sobbing on the doorstep as this woman took me, still screaming, through the town to a dirt road that led into a dark, heavily wooded forest just beyond the town's streets. She walked all afternoon, carrying me, despite all my protests.

Although I cried all the way, I finally grew tired and stopped resisting. I couldn't understand any of it, least of all the necessity of being torn from my parents. The sun slipped lower in the sky above us as we walked along that little road beneath the towering trees and their deepening shadows until, at twilight, we came to a small, decaying hut in a little clearing in the woods. She put me into a tiny room with one small window and I stared out at the forest, imagining my parents were watching me from behind the huge tree trunks that surrounded the clearing. I was four years old.

The forest in which I found myself had a haunting beauty that remains with me to this day. But life there never seemed entirely real. In the warm months I lived almost entirely in the woods, wandering about amidst the trees and brooks, coming back only at night to sleep in one of the little rooms on a small cot that was provided for me. I ate wild berries that I picked myself and played by making "strawberry trees" from denuded pine branches which I threaded with tiny wild strawberries. I wandered the forest with these branches in my hands and often lay on the hillsides, watching the clouds. Sometimes I went back to the hut and ate something there in the evenings. I had very little contact with the people who had taken me in. It was a lonely life for a small child who, despite the enchantment of a seemingly magical forest, could never stop pining for her parents.

Janek, the man who took care of me, roamed the forest for his Nazi employers. He returned every few weeks carrying a string of small animals he had trapped. These supplemented our food supply. I helped him hang his catch on a branch near the hut and skin them. We had a few chickens, too, and I would hold their necks across a stump while Magda, who also lived there with Janek, chopped their heads off with an ax. Janek always wore his uniform and high boots, carrying a rifle at his shoulder. He was the Nazis' forest watchman. He always slept on a cot near me when he was with us.

The hut, itself, was small and shabby. It was entirely built of rough trimmed wood with a floor-to-ceiling Russian stove to warm its two rooms. Every morning Magda, who was very superstitious, would open the stove door and read calamity for us in the hot, glowing coals. I only slept when it rained, fearing the house would burn down around me and I would not be able to escape because, by then, I'd have broken my leg carrying water from the nearby stream to Magda, so she could use it for drinking and cooking.

There was no toilet in the hut; we had to go outside for that purpose. On a small back porch there was a mountain of feces, infested with flies and wriggling white worms. I, too, soon had nits, lice and white worms on me.

The long winter came and snow covered the little windows of the hut. No sunlight ever melted the frost "flowers" that sprouted from the cold upon the windowpanes. The rooms remained in perpetual twilight. When we opened the door, a burst of dazzling whiteness would blind me. I stayed indoors throughout the winter—no shoes, no coat. Stasia, Magda's four year old daughter, remained near her mother and I lived alone in the dark corners. Magda paid little attention to me.

With spring came the Nazis, walking on the road in twos and threes. Stefan, Janek's brother, came to us one day from a village outside the forest. He and Janek sat around a little wooden table talking. A Christian family had been murdered that morning, he said, together with the Jews they had been hiding. "You must take her out to the forest in the morning and shoot her," Stefan told Janek gravely. "She's too dangerous to keep here any longer."

"What if her parents return?" asked Janek. "What can I say to them?"

"They will never come back," Stefan said.

They spoke like this in front of me, and that night I slept until the twilight of the next day, dreaming all the while that I was already dead. When I finally awoke again I felt my arm to reassure myself that I was still alive.

Stefan came to the hut in the forest many times afterwards and he and Janek spoke among themselves often, but Janek never acted on Stefan's urgent request.

There were times when they took me away, to stay with a woman in the town of Lwow. There I attended church regularly with her but mostly she kept me out of sight, hidden from others. Still, her neighbors eventually became suspicious and, after a time, Janek brought me back to the forest. In the nights I dreamt of endless tunnels beneath gnarled trees through which I ran and ran and ran. In the hut I was silent and still.

The seasons passed and, after a time, I began to see flaming bombs as they fell over the distant horizon beyond the trees of our forest, the gray clouds rising in plumes of incendiary smoke where they struck. The bombs soon fell relentlessly every afternoon and I continued to watch them daily from the crest of a hill.

One afternoon, as I held a chicken down over a tree stump with Magda poised above it, ax in hand, she suddenly turned and said, "Look down the road."

I looked and saw Stefan coming toward us with a woman beside him, walking slowly, haltingly. The woman was very thin. I thought I knew her. When they reached us I broke from Magda and the squawking chicken and ran to them.

My mother smiled down at me, tears welling from her eyes and dampening her face. Some fell and touched my cheeks, too, and I cried with her. She had brought a little blue raincoat and she wrapped me tenderly in it. Two years and a terrible war that had kept us apart were gone.

The man who saved our lives, mine and especially my parents, Jozef Zwonarz, was a person of many facets. He was the youngest of six children ... four brothers and two sisters. His father, Adalbert Zwonarz, a respected mechanic in his community, died when Jozef, or Józio as he was always known to us, was only five years old. Józio's mother, a Hungarian, took her children to Budapest and there Józio grew up, learning Hungarian and German, the language of the Austro-Hungarian Empire under the Emperor Franz Jozef. German would prove useful to him later in life.

Józio studied engineering in Budapest but did not receive his diploma, volunteering, instead, to serve in the Hungarian army with his brother Wilhelm when the First World War broke out. After the war and the break-up of the Austro-Hungarian Empire, Józio returned to Poland and settled in the town of Lesko on the river San. He worked at various jobs and ultimately opened a workshop on Grunwaldzka Street in the center of Lesko, where he installed and maintained all sorts of engines, electrical generators and similar equipment. He became well known and took on apprentices, young men from all parts of the community including Poles, Jews and Ukrainians. We came to know him because my grandfather, Josef Manaster, needed his skilled hand on our farm in the nearby village of Orelec. Józio was often there because of this and became fast friends with my uncles, Pinek and Milek.

In 1937 my father opened a medical practice in Sanok on the other side of the San River. Józio was a frequent guest in our home there. I was born in 1938. By 1939, with war fast approaching, Józio was mobilized, and sent to the front to defend Poland. But he never fought in the conflict. His unit quickly retreated eastwards as the German army advanced. They were apprehended on the Polish/Soviet border by the Russians and, since no one in the unit identified himself as the person in charge, the Russians checked the soldiers' hands. Seeing Józio's were rough and calloused, they presumed he was a simple foot soldier. They released him and sent him home.

Józio had married Franciszka Yadlowska, from a very old Leskian family and was fully accepted by the townspeople there because of this. During the subsequent Russian occupation, Franciszka's family was actually interned by the Russians in Siberia because one of her uncles had escaped to Belgium when taken prisoner-of-war by the Germans. This cast a pall of suspicion on the entire family. But Franciszka, whom we called Franka, was spared because her marriage to Józio gave her a new surname, making her a Zwonarz.

When my parents were faced with the Nazi disaster, it was Józio who came to their aid, finding a way to save me and to hide them for as long as the Nazis were in control. Of the roughly 30,000 Jews in the area there were only about eighty survivors at the end of the war. I was the only child who lived.

During all the time Józio hid my parents and uncles, at great risk to his own life and to the lives of his family, he maintained his workshop where he fixed Nazi vehicles and machines. His behavior was that of a shiftless, though proficient, mechanic and a harmless fool. All the while he pretended to be friendly to the Germans but he was rushing about behind the scenes, earning extra food with his labor in nearby peasants' fields, pilfering what he could, to keep my parents and uncles alive. After the war, when we were able to move about again, he gave my parents the little money he had kept for them and a gold watch he said he no longer needed.

But my parents saw that there was no future in Poland for us anymore, or in any part of Europe, and so they finally made their way to America. They arrived in May of 1947 and in that same year, in the fall, they received Józio's first letter:

*Lesko, 27.11.1947*
*My dear friends,*

*We were very happy to hear from you. We have not forgotten our shared experience; it feels like a nightmare, and yet it gives us great joy that our shared suffering had a happy ending. Thank God we are all alive and in good health.*

*I have registered my workshop only last January and am slowly beginning to work; we are not very well off, but things are improving. I'll try to get the photographs of your hideout which you had asked for. I believe that it would be worthwhile to describe it all in a form of a memoir in the American press, so it is not forgotten.*

*Here is still winter, but the sun shines, so it might soon get warmer.*

*The kind of problem which you refer to is still with us, yet it only serves to confirm our satisfaction that in spite of all the great difficulties we had lived through, we can now feel we had done our duty and fulfilled our aims, if not perfectly, then at least in a satisfactory manner. The best prize we can hope for is to hear that you are happy in your present life. We would like to go on doing good deeds, provided our health allows it.*

*Our children are doing well in school. Isia is in 3rd grade of the middle school, while Janka attends the 6th. Zosia the 3rd grade of the primary school and Franek and Lusia are still at home.*

*I live in hope that we shall yet be together and enjoy each other's company again. I pray to God that we should have peace in the world at last.*

*Poor little Rena, does she still remember that Christmas tree? Tears fill my eyes when I remember all that we have been through together.*

*My wife's family has returned from Russia and, thank God, they have all survived. That is all.*

*May I just add my best regards, a handshake, a kiss for the lady's hand and a special kiss for Rena, my little martyr. I shall write more next time.*

*Your sincere friend,*
*Józio*

In 1949 the Communists consolidated power in Poland and Józio's workshop was nationalized. Local papers wrote of Józio that "he has ceased to be a relic of Capitalism and is now proof that a system of oppression of man by man has been replaced by a better one." He had ceased to be a "bloodsucker," they wrote.

Though Józio continued to survive by managing a state school for construction, where he taught young people his skills, he lost all enthusiasm for his work. Later, he became very embittered when Franka, his wife, was arrested for listening to Christmas carols on Radio Free Europe. She was interned for a long time, perhaps because Józio had become an outspoken critic of Communist policies by then.

In 1956, with the "October thaw" in Poland, Józio got his workshop back. But where he had once worked with as many as 17 assistants and laborers, many of whom he had saved from deportation to the Reich, he now worked alone. My parents stayed in touch with him during this period and sent him money through the good offices of a Polish-American professor who frequently went back to that country. They also sent packages of clothing, shoes and other necessities since life under the Communists was not easy and these things were hard to come by.

In 1980, after years of advocacy by my parents and others, Józio was allowed to travel to Belgium where he received a medal honoring his efforts to save us. The medal was presented by Dr. Moshe Bejski, the head of the Justice Committee of Yad Vashem, Israel's Center for Holocaust Remembrance in Jerusalem. The ceremony was held at the Israeli Consulate in Brussels to which the European press had been invited. It was well attended. Józio's son, Romauld, told me years later that his father, on receiving the award, said that "It's better to get a medal for saving one person, than for killing thousands."

Although my parents had planned for a long delayed reunion with Józio when he finally received his medal, they were, in the end, unable to attend. My father had been blinded in a motor vehicle accident four years earlier in Israel, where they had been living since 1963. My father was 71 at the time and had just retired from his position in a government medical clinic. He had dreams of studying philosophy, his great love, at the University of Haifa for the remainder of his life. But in a freak accident he was thrown onto the rail of a pick-up truck on which he had hitched a ride, smashing his nose and eyes.

The accident had been caused by a young man on a motorcycle who had sped into the road in front of the truck, causing the driver of the pick-up to stop short. The young man on the motorcycle, a German volunteer who had come to Israel to atone, in his words, for the crimes of his countrymen, was so distraught by what had occurred that he stayed by my mother throughout the subsequent ordeal. First in Rambam Hospital in Haifa and later at Hadassah

Hospital in Jerusalem, this young German remained with her, consoling her as best he could and hoping with her that my father's eyes could be saved. But they could not and Werner, the young man, committed suicide when he learned of this. When Józio heard what had happened he wrote to my mother: "I would give ten years of my life for Natan to see again," he said.

My father became very depressed as a result of the accident and his rehabilitation was long and arduous. He never learned to walk alone with a cane or to master Braille. My mother had to be his eyes. For the next twenty years of their life together, until my father's death at the age of ninety, she cared for him with single-minded devotion.

Although my parents had moved to Israel in 1963, to fulfill a lifelong dream, we had initially settled in the United States. Arriving in America in 1947, my father had opened a medical practice in a community called Arverne on the Rockaway peninsula in New York City. My mother had sewn my father's medical diploma from the German University of Prague into her girdle and so had successfully carried it with them all the way to America. In 1948 my brother Sheldon was born. Today Sheldon lives in Arizona with his family. He works in Customer Service for a large retail company.

Because my parents had long dreamed of living in Israel, they resettled there, with Sheldon, in 1963. That move brought my parents great satisfaction and, until my father's accident in 1976, they were quite happy. While once walking with my mother in a rundown section of Haifa, I remember her turning to me and saying, with visible pride: "See, we're a country now. We have our own prostitutes and vagrants, just like all the other nations of the world." My parents took a special delight in being a part of the new Jewish state and in seeing Hebrew restored to the world as a living, breathing language.

Józio died in 1984 of cancer. We had not seen him again since those terrible days and news of his passing was a blow to us. My uncles, Pinek and Milek, settled in Sao Paulo, Brazil after the war where they opened a sweater factory together and prospered for a time. Milek, who had always tortured himself over his inability to save others in our family, died of a heart attack in 1967 while still a relatively young man. My mother said it was a broken heart.

Pinek eventually relocated with his family to Haifa, Israel, and I met him there again after many years. He was a remote and pessimistic man, very difficult to talk to. He died in 2002. Hela, my aunt, finally came to America from Warsaw in 1968 though Norbert, her husband, did not follow. She, too, was gloomy and pessimistic, tormented by her past. She died in 2001. My mother's youngest sister, Anna, lost her husband in a car accident in 1979 and still lives in Far Rockaway, New York, very much alone.

In 1991 my parents left Haifa, Israel and settled in Rockville, Maryland...a suburb of Washington, DC. My aunt Helena, my mother's younger sister, resided in an assisted living facility called Revits House...and my parents joined her there. My father died in 1995. Mother stayed in Revits House until my aunt's death in 2002. She then came to live near me in Brooklyn, New York.

My mother was the most wonderful, wise and kind person I have ever known. She died in 2011 at the age of 101.

The large and extended family we all left behind in Poland, in those terrible years, lives on for us now only in our words and our prayers.

# Photographs

*Leibish Manaster, Jafa Wallach's grandfather
in the early 20th century.*

*Josef Manaster (ca. 1939).
He died in Belżec, a Nazi
death camp, in 1943.
He lost his second wife,
Sarah, and three of his
children and their families
in Belżec.*

*Rachel Manaster, mother
of Jafa Wallach, before her
death in 1935.*

*Josef Manaster with some of his children and their families at the farm in Orelec, just before the Soviet takeover in 1939.*

*Natan Wallach and his two sisters, Sala and Hania, and a cousin (ca. 1920's).*

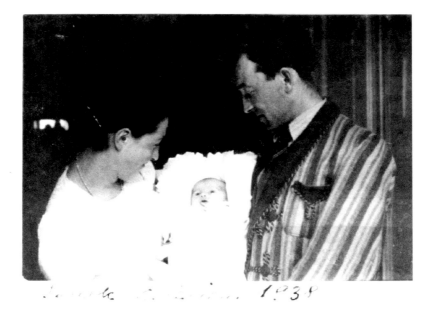

*Rena, a few days old, with her parents, Natan and Jafa Wallach,*
*in Sanok, Poland, April 1938.*

*Jafa Wallach holding her newly born daughter, Rena, with her
sister, Bronka Manaster (on the right) in May, 1938.*

*Branka Manaster (ca. 1937) saved hundreds of people
from deportation to Siberia by the Soviets in 1940.
She died in Belżec in 1943.*

*Natan Wallach as he appeared under the Russian occupation
in Stryj, Poland, ca. 1940.*

*Natan Wallach in his medical office in Sanok, ca. 1938.*

*Józef Zwonarz (Józio) in 1939.*

*The workshop in the center of Lesko in which Józef Zwonarz kept five people alive under the very noses of the Gestapo and the Ukranian Militia.*

*The entrance to the cellar where Jafa Wallach, her husband and two brothers hid for almost two years. With the help of Józef Zwonarz they constructed a man-made cave 1.9 meters by 1.4 meters. Standing on their knees, their heads struck the wooden board that sealed them in.*

*Rena in Lwów, ca. 1942.*  *Janek Konkol's fiancée, Wilka, in Lwów, ca. 1943. She protected and hid Rena Wallach Bernstein under the Nazi occupation in 1942.*

*Four year old Rena in Wilka's house in Lwów, ca. 1942, with two unknown friends.*

*Wilka (left) with Stasia and Janek in front of the house in Bezmiechowa,*

*Rena with Janek and Wilka (right), ca. 1943.*

*Magda with mother and brother, Stasia (left) and Rena in Bezmiechowa, ca. 1943.*

*Anna Manaster stayed in Bezmiechowa with Rena (left) for five weeks. Finally, in 1944, she sought refuge in Józef Zwonarz's cellar in Lesko with her sister and brothers.*

*Rena and Stasia, ca. 1944.*

*Stefan Konkol (left), Janek Konkol (right) with their father and Rena in 1943. This photo was taken in the forest of Bezmiechowa, where the Konkols hid the little girl from the Nazis for two years.*

*The day Jafa Wallach was reunited with her daughter after the liberation of Lesko, ca. 1944.*

*Magda, Stasia, Rena and Jafa Wallach on their first day together.*

*Natan and Jafa Wallach with their daughter Rena in Rome, ca. 1946.*

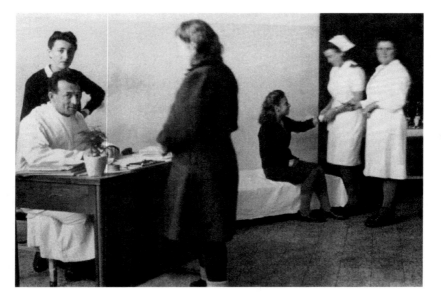

*Natan Wallach in the Polish camp clinic in Barletta, Italy ca. 1946.*

*Above (right) is Anna Manaster leaning on the gravestone
of her mother, Rachel Manaster, ca. 1946.
Below is the cemetery as it appeared in 1993.*

*Arriving in New York harbor in May 1947: The Wallachs—Jafa, Natan and Rena—are pictured on the last voyage of the Italian battleship Saturnia.*

*Jafa Wallach, in the early
'60s, in Haifa, Israel.*

*Helena Manaster Ramer in America in the 1970s.
Her story is told in the Appendix to this book.*

*The medal awarded to Józef Zwonarz, honoring him as one of the Righteous Gentiles Among the Nations, for saving Jews during World War II. The medal was awarded to him by Dr. Moshe Bejski of the Justice Committee of Yad Vashem in Jerusalem. He received it in the Israeli Consulate in Brussels, Belgium in 1980.*

*Rena Wallach Bernstein standing in front of the great synagogue
in Lesko when she returned to Poland for a visit in 1993.
The building was empty except for a paper scroll taped to one
wall recording the names of the Jews of Lesko who had died at the
hands of the Nazis. She found many members of her extended
family on the scroll.*

*Polish borders during World War II before and after
the joint German-Soviet invasion.*

# Appendix

# THE STORY OF
# HELENA MANASTER RAMER

I was born in Poland in a small town called Lesko in 1917. I grew up and attended school there. On summer vacations I always came back to our family's home, an estate near Lesko which my father had built up from very little in the village of Orelec. We were all on summer vacation there when the war broke out on September 1, 1939. My father had begun purchasing the properties that made up our home right after World War I. He was a businessman who bought and sold land. He kept several houses in Lesko and Przemysl, too. Because of his hard work and acumen, we were very well off.

Ours was a large family. I was one of ten brothers and sisters, three boys and seven girls. I was the eighth child. By 1939, some of my sisters and my older brother were already married and had moved away, living with families of their own. But at vacation time we all came together at my father's house. Unfortunately, my mother had died in 1935 but my father had remarried and so we had a stepmother to care for us. We all got along with our stepmother and understood that our father was still a young man.

We hadn't been home more than a month when the Russians came and "nationalized" our home. They simply threw us out and did not permit us to take even an extra pair of shoes when we left. Our servants were good people and brought us some of our things secretly, in the first few days of our eviction. Then it was the beginning of October. The eastern half of Poland was occupied by the Russians and the western part by Germany. The dividing line between the two areas fell exactly where we lived, along the San River. Lesko, our town, was on the Russian side in the east and Sanok, the next large town, was on the western side, under the Germans.

We made our way to Lwow, the closest big city in the east, farther into Russian territory and tried to re-establish our home there. My father, Josef Manaster, was not used to big city life, nor were we children. But we were young and began to adjust. Once the initial dislocations were behind us, life seemed to quiet down under the Russian occupiers. We took jobs and I worked in a Russian office. My first typing job was on a Russian typewriter and it wasn't hard to learn because it was so similar to Ukrainian, one of the three languages we all learned simultaneously as children. Because of where we lived, we had to speak Polish and Ukrainian both and, of course, we learned Yiddish among our own.

Unfortunately, the quiet times we had found in Lwow did not last long. Someone had denounced my father to the authorities and he had to flee again, to a small place outside of the city. While in Lwow, I married Norbert Ramer. He was a very highly educated man, a medical doctor and doctor of mathematics. He was also a rabbi.

In June 1941 the Russians and Germans abrogated their peace treaty and went to war. It took the Germans only a week to drive the Russians out and enter Lwow. No one expected this. The Russians seemed to have been caught completely off guard and quickly retreated. Whoever could go with them did so. It was the smartest thing to do.

We Jews had heard about the German persecutions, but most of us didn't believe it. Many Jews who had come from the west to escape the Germans initially had actually registered with the Russian authorities to go back there in order to reunite with their families. They didn't care for life under the Russians. But before these people could return to the German zone, the Russians sent them to Siberia.

Unfortunately, we didn't follow the Russians when they retreated before the German advance and were still in Lwow when the Nazis came. The new authorities were more dreadful than the old. When the holiday for a Ukrainian hero named Petlura arrived, soon after the Germans came, it became an excuse to commence persecuting Jews. It was the occasion for the first "action" against us. The day after, we heard that many thousands of Jews were taken away and never heard from again. Soon after this we couldn't even walk freely in the street or get food. We still lived in the same apartment but a ghetto was being prepared for us and we were told we would have to move there. This was in November. They took our money, furs, jewelry—anything of value that we had managed to preserve. The *Judenraat* had to collect and deliver everything any Jew still had that was of value and a penalty of death was imposed for hiding money or furs.

We decided to go back to Lesko before they pushed us into the ghetto. Since the whole area was now occupied by the Nazis, it didn't matter where you were. My husband found someone to drive us there and we paid a high price, a piece of jewelry from what we had managed to hide. The rest of my family was already in Lesko. Some of my siblings were medical students and my husband was already a doctor, having passed his exams. He got official papers from the Nazis to settle in one of the villages to fight a typhus epidemic that was then taking hold and I went along as his nurse.

We went there in November and stayed through the winter … until June. Things were quiet in the village. We cared for the sick and were paid with potatoes or grain. In June there was another "action" against the Jews, but we were not at home at the time because we were attending to the sick child of the Ukrainian village headman. The few Jewish families that lived in that village along with us were working in the fields, spreading manure.

The Ukrainians were very helpful to the Nazis. When told to throw Jews out of their houses and collect the valuables, they did. Told to bring all the Jews to a town hall in a neighboring village, they did this too. As soon as we returned we were rounded up and taken to the designated building, about 150 people from all the surrounding villages. They held us there for a day without food or water. Then the Gestapo arrived and "registered" everyone. When they saw that Norbert, my husband, was a doctor, they allowed him to go and permitted me to accompany him as his nurse. But they would not release his mother and he didn't want to leave her. I tried to convince him that, if we stayed, we were all lost. "As long as we're free to go," I said, "let's take advantage of it. Maybe the *Judenraat* can help us." They were still active in the town. Finally, he agreed and we left.

Later we learned they had murdered everyone who remained that very night. The Judenraat did nothing. They killed them all. We knew then that eventually we would be killed, but we still hoped to find a way to survive.

Trying to return to our village, we saw Gestapo heading our way and hid ourselves. They must have realized that whoever had been released would be witnesses to what they had done. My husband had a cousin, a well-known doctor in Sosnica, so we tried to go there. Since most traveling was now forbidden, we had to be very careful. We went to Lesko and got papers from a doctor there that said I was sick due to a miscarriage and had to be hospitalized. Then we got a ride in another car, paying very dearly for it with another piece of the jewelry I had hung onto.

In Przemysl, the major town in the area where we now went, there was no ghetto as yet. It was a big place with maybe 150,000 inhabitants and many Ukrainians in the area nearby. This was in the southern part of Poland.

Norbert's cousin put me in the hospital, though none of us realized the danger that the sick and old were already beginning to be liquidated. I rubbed the thermometer when the nurses took my temperature, raising the reading in order to remain there for as long as I could.

When I was finally discharged, we stayed with Norbert's cousin a few days but a ghetto was even then being constructed around us. Because our host was a famous surgeon, he had a fair-sized apartment with two rooms, maybe three—this when other Jews were living seven families to a room. Jews in the neighboring towns were being rounded up and brought to Przemysl and pushed into the ghetto with us. There were maybe 100,000 people or more in the congested area.

Another "action" soon began and 30,000 people were taken away. They told us it was for resettlement. The people they took were told to bring enough food, water and some soap for two weeks. Everyone believed it. We never thought this would be the end. It was only later that we learned of the gas chambers.

Norbert got permission to remain in Przemysl, so we weren't taken in that "action." Many of our neighbors and friends and a lot of others I knew from other places went though. It was an awful thing to watch as these people gathered at the umshlagplatz. I can still see them now. How can I say what my thoughts were then? My heart went out to them and I felt guilty that I was able to remain and they could not. They took them away in cattle cars to the nearest extermination camp, but we didn't know that until afterwards.

Because I was in the ghetto at Przemysl I had lost all contact with my father, brothers and sisters, all of whom were still in Lesko. They ended up in the Zaslaw camp a few kilometers from

Lesko—every one of them. I didn't know what happened to them and those who lived didn't know what had happened to me until after the war. I had last seen them in 1942.

Of course the Przemysl Ghetto got smaller as they took people away. As the people were taken away, they moved the ghetto walls, pressing us ever more tightly together. There was hunger, sickness, and crying children and mothers all the time now in the ghetto, and many "actions." Each "action" took away more of the children and elderly, along with the sick who were in the hospitals. During some of these "actions" we found hiding places. Once we hid ourselves in a cellar. Several families were with us. We covered the door to our hiding place with a cupboard. Soon we heard the Germans walking around above us, looking for us. But they didn't find our door, which is how we survived. That time.

Norbert's cousin was no longer there with us. He had been able to obtain false papers for himself, his wife and his children, making them out to be Poles. He got papers for Norbert and me, too, but we didn't have any money and lacked the courage to leave. Where could we go? It was hard to get out of the ghetto, though people could sometimes do it by bribing the guards. We, however, had nothing left with which to bribe them. Our cousin's sister had also remained in the ghetto with her family and now she told us they knew someone in Lwow who could hide them, some German Poles. We had nothing left to lose and so we pulled ourselves together and fled with them. But when we arrived in Lwow, in the middle of the night, things turned out badly. The people we had traveled with returned disappointed from the family they had hoped would take them. The family had refused. We were very scared. It was night and we were Jews with false papers and no money. Norbert and I decided to return to Przemysl and the ghetto.

There were more "actions" all the time in Przemysl now and some people would commit suicide when they heard of what was coming, especially the old. By this time people knew what these "actions" meant. They knew what awaited them. People who couldn't kill themselves got others to do it for them. I remember a person in our building who injected air into his elderly father's vein. It was the easiest way to do it. A Dr. Vilcher killed his mother-in-law in the same way. It was horrible, to kill your own mother and father in order to help them avoid death at the hands of the Germans. Unburied dead lay everywhere now in the streets.

We were there at the last "action" in Przemysl, and after that they organized the people who were left into a workshop. We were included because we were still fit. At the workshop they announced that they needed a doctor to go to a labor camp between Przemysl and Radimo, a small town near Sosnica. Norbert volunteered. I went with him as his assistant. At the camp we fought typhus again and were among the privileged ones, privileged because they allowed us to sleep in the clinic, not among the prisoners, privileged because they allowed us to live. We secretly carried our Polish papers with us.

It was the beginning of November when we arrived at the camp which held some 200 men who were used to work on a pipeline that was being built. We had to wear Star of David armbands identifying us as Jews. We also wore a letter "R" on our lapels. People were dying there like flies and we did what we could for them. Men who were tall and robust in appearance one moment were suddenly dead the next.

We were issued something they called "coffee" and ten grams of bread in the morning, some soup in a kettle for lunch and in the evenings. Some young people who were there worked in the villages and sometimes they brought us back a little food. During this time we were allowed to go into the town. People who saw me there in the streets often took me in and gave me food. I was able to spend a few hours with them. They were Poles but they sympathized with our situation. I took what they gave me but not too much because, if I did, the guards would confiscate it when I came back to the camp. I brought back whatever I could, a small contribution to the men who would come begging me for food.

They frequently had "selections" at the camp at which the sick, the weak and all those who were deemed no longer able to work would be killed. When I close my eyes now, I can still see a young man running into the clinic as they were taking them to the "resolution" location. "Doctor, doctor," he begged us, "help me. Save me." We could do nothing. It was horrible. I live with these memories, even today.

On the 18th of February the Gestapo came. They began to record everyone's name and to take everything we still had in our possession. We learned they were to liquidate us the following morning. The work on the pipeline was done. What else do you do with people after you're finished with them but kill them?

The camp was closed and they locked us in the clinic. We were in a small room with a barred window. The next room was occupied by the camp leader, a German. Beyond that room was a very large hall which served as the police station. There were four policemen, all Ukrainian. They watched us all night and opened the doors several times to make sure we were still there. We had no way out. We waited, knowing that in the morning it would be the end. I had a bit of gray hair and I told Norbert that I had read a story of someone's hair turning white in a single night. He just stared at me.

We waited. We didn't sleep. After a time we heard someone's radio from beyond the wall. It was Goebbel's voice, speaking about a breakthrough in the siege of Stalingrad. Because it was winter it was still dark at seven o'clock in the morning and the guards were all tired after watching us through the night. As we watched through our little window we saw one guard go out in the direction of the prisoners' barracks—probably going to have breakfast. There seemed to be only one man left. He opened the door and looked in on us and then left, locking the door again behind him. Norbert whispered to me that now was our chance.

"We've got to escape," he said. Norbert had a second key to the door which he had gotten from the former occupant of the clinic.

When he handed it to Norbert he had said, "Keep it, you never know when you'll need it." Norbert waited till everything was quiet and then went to the door and opened it. I followed him and we ran to the outer door, but it was locked. Norbert grabbed hold of the lock and worked at it desperately while I looked around, frightened, afraid we would be heard. Somehow he managed to pull it open. We ran out into the darkness.

I was only half-dressed and it was cold, the snow deep. We made our way to the man who had given Norbert the extra key and he hurriedly offered me a babushka and some food. It kept me warm, at least. We couldn't remain there any longer, of course. We tore off our armbands and the "R" signs we had been forced to wear and buried them in a heap of snow. Then we started walking, just walking. I don't know how many miles we traveled. It was just a long, long way. We had no money, nothing. We walked until we came to a village. Later we learned it was Sosnica. It was inhabited mainly by Ukrainians, but we had no choice. We went to one house and said we were merchants and had come to purchase food. That house belonged to a Polish man. We later learned that there were only four Polish families in the entire village, so we were lucky in our choice. We told him we wanted to buy food but had no money with us. He let us stay for a time and gave us something to eat and drink.

Later our host went into the village and when he came back he told us something was going on there. "There's a lot of commotion," he said. He looked at us strangely. "They say the doctor and nurse have run away from the camp and they're looking for them. I don't know who you are. You're not doctors; you're strangers, so you'd better leave."

We asked him for directions to the train station, hoping to take a train back to Przemysl. He said it was far outside the village and gave us directions. We left. We discovered there was only one train each day.

When we got to the station it was already three o'clock in the afternoon. We had been walking in the snow for most of the day but we knew they would tear us to pieces if they caught us. We sat down in the train station as people began to come in. They told us the Germans had surrounded the village, checking everyone. They were hunting us, we learned, with dogs.

At around six o'clock the train finally came and we boarded it without a ticket. If the train station had not been so far outside the village we would have been out of luck. We had no money but we took it to Przemysl and no one interfered. Although we made our way to Norbert's cousin, who was now living under false papers, he wasn't at home. His wife took us in and let us remain there overnight. But in the middle of the night Norbert's cousin returned. He was furious to see us there, thinking we had come to collect our things, which he didn't want to give to us. If we didn't leave immediately, he told us, he would denounce us. We agreed to go. He took us to the train station and we took a train to Krakow.

The Polish papers we had previously secured and hidden with us proved valuable. I became Helena Dabrowski and Norbert, Tadeusz Dabrowski, two Polish nationals. We were on that train all night and into the following day. German officials came through, searching for kielbasa and ham, anything people might be hiding illicitly. We didn't have any of that and, in fact, had very little of anything at that point. When we arrived in Krakow I was lost, but my husband had studied mathematics there and had many acquaintances and friends. We went at once to the home of one of these, a bachelor, and he took us in. After all these years I've forgotten his name, but he kept us with him for three days. Norbert got in touch with other friends and we made contact with the underground. We also managed to get a little money so that we could get by.

We were no longer Jews, however. We lived in different skins. Someone urged me to smile more and I did my best. We had to smile all the time, to remain above suspicion. We just walked the streets, smiling, and all the time I wanted to cry because I saw Jews on the streets going to work. There was a camp for Jews near Krakow and many were still allowed to leave with work passes. Where else could they go with the Nazis in control of everything?

By this time it was February 1943 and I was pregnant. Still Norbert and I remained apart as much as possible to avoid suspicion. While I didn't look Jewish, Norbert had a more difficult time and had to spend much of his time indoors when he could. We found places to sleep, but it was always harder to find places to spend the days and in the spring and summer the days were so long. We walked in the parks and in the stores and banks. We spent hours in the churches. We generally went to the churches to meet. Sometimes, too, we met in the waiting rooms of local doctors. Some people knew who we were and were even helpful to us.

At that time there was an 8 o'clock curfew and you had to be off the streets after that hour. All our efforts in the days were directed at finding places for the nights. Sometimes we even found places where we could stay in the daytime, too. Then we could bathe and get some food. At one point we were in contact with a gynecologist Norbert knew. She was aware that we were Jewish, but didn't want to make trouble for us. She told me, "It's easier for you to survive being pregnant. No one will suspect you of being a Jew. But if they do, if you have to die, you'll die pregnant. What's the difference?"

"How will I give birth to the child?" I said. "Where will I go? Where will I spend the nights?"

"Have faith," she answered me. "I know how to do it when the time comes."

But as time progressed, I worried more and more. Then, one day, I found myself in a difficult situation. I had an arrangement on that day to spend the following night with some people, but I had nowhere to go that night. I couldn't wait until the following evening so I went to the people who were supposed to take me in the next night, right then and there, even though I wasn't supposed to. I was afraid and went to their apartment just at curfew, hoping they wouldn't throw me out.

They were having a party and I couldn't go inside because I didn't want to be seen by too many people. So I sat in the hallway of their building, in an old chair that I found there, instead. There were two apartments in that hallway, one occupied by a university professor who was a known antisemite. I was very worried. At that time, many Poles were being executed by the Nazis in the east and there were many orphans. The professor's daughter, it turned out, was the head nurse of an organization that was engaged in rescuing these children. While I was sitting there she came out and saw me, pregnant, in the chair, in the middle of the night, and asked who I was. I told her my husband lived in Hungary and that I had nowhere to go. Her face softened and she offered to help me. What could I say? What else was there to do? She took me to a monastery that night.

She took me to the Order of the Capuchin. They had several buildings in Krakow and a vast garden. One of the buildings was being used to house refugees and the sick. They put me there. I stayed in that place for almost two years and that's where my son Arthur was born. As our gynecologist friend had said, "Have faith." Finding that professor's daughter proved a great and unbelievable blessing to me, though I don't believe she ever knew that I was a Jew.

While there, I arranged to go to the hospital when I was due to give birth. The manager of the refugees house, a pious young man named Mr. Detz, took me. My son was born in October, but he took sick soon after I returned with him to the monastery and I had to take him back to the hospital for care several times. I had named him Tadeusz, but in my mind he was always Arthur. People at the monastery thought he might die and urged me to baptize him so he would not die a pagan and, finally, I did. I was afraid to keep refusing. It was now July and I began to hope we would survive by remaining in the monastery. I got money from the underground, but I spent very little and lived there for almost two years.

The nurse who had placed me in the monastery came to visit sometimes and, at one point, asked me to raise another baby as well. I agreed. Krysia was three weeks old when they brought her to me and I cared for her, a beautiful and healthy girl, until she was six months old. Then I had to leave her. Once a German came over to me as I was sitting with the children in the garden and I became very frightened. I thought he had come for me, but he only complimented me on the children and left.

Later a more serious incident occurred. I found something that looked like a crudely made mezuzah, the little ornamental box containing a prayer that is put on the doorways of Jewish homes. It had been placed in the night on my doorpost. Someone was telling me that they knew what I was. It was then May 1944 and I had been in Krakow since February 1943. One evening, Mr. Detz, the manager, came to see me and said, "You can't stay here any longer. Two of our patients are going to denounce the Jews we are hiding here.

This was the first time that I realized I was not the only Jew at the monastery. One of the older men there, a man who used to visit me quite often and tell me stories of how he always prayed to Jesus and the Virgin Mary and relied on their help for everything, was a Jew, too. Mr. Detz said I had to leave at once.

I had retained contact with the underground and one of them, a Miss Eiserle, took me in. Her father was a Polish officer in exile in England, but her mother was a Jew and in hiding. I left little Krysia behind and went to Miss Eiserle but I had to leave soon after arriving. I now took Arthur from place to place in the six months remaining until the liberation in January 1945. We were here a week, there a week, in places the underground arranged for us. Often I would come to an apartment but find no one home. I would wait on the stairs for many hours, the baby crying, without food or diapers to change him. Once some German police came and demanded my identity papers. By this time I was no longer Helena Dabrowski. I now had a paper from a place already occupied by the Russians so they couldn't check it, but the paper was not very convincing and, had they checked closely, would have been seen as a forgery. They looked me over and asked for something else, but I had no other identity papers, having destroyed the old ones to prevent their discovery. They sent me to the police station where I was told by the officer in charge to "come back tomorrow with your papers and bring someone you know to vouch for you."

One of my husband's friends, a doctor, went back there with me and testified on my behalf. It was a very risky thing for him to do.

It was almost the end of the war and we had survived. But the Polish resistance had made a lot of trouble for the Germans and the Nazis' revenge was horrible. People were grabbed in the streets and hung from lamp posts right then and there. There were dead bodies hanging throughout the streets of Krakow and Warsaw and in all the big cities. We tried not to go outside.

Liberation came to us on January 17th, 1945.

My father, stepmother and three of my sisters had been murdered in Belzec in January 1943. My brother Muniu and his family and my sister Esther, with her family, were murdered, too. We don't know where or how, to this day, but my sister Sabina, who took the Hebrew name Jafa, later wrote about how she and some others of my family managed to survive in Lesko. My brothers Milek and Pinek and my sister Anna survived together with Sabina and her husband Natan, hiding like animals in a hole in the dirt beneath the ground. I lived with death and the smell of death all around me in those years, too.

# BIBLIOGRAPHY

Gilbert, Sir Martin. *Holocaust*. NY: Holt, Rinehart and Winston, 1985.

Gilbert, Sir Martin. *The Holocaust Maps and Photographs*. Jerusalem: Jerusalem Post Publishers, 1978.

Frontline PBS "Shtetl Biographies"
http://www.pbs.org/wgbh/pages/frontline/shtetl/righteous/gentilesbios.html

"NAAF Holocaust Project Timeline 1943."
http://www.neveragain.org/1943.html

"Polish Righteous"
http://www.raoul-Wallenberg,org.ar/english/Saviors/POLONIA/kv.html

Rosenfield, Anita. "Traveling The Road Together: Righteous Among the Nations"
http://www.sedonajewishcommunity.org/Newsletter_%_2005_06June/index.vds?Article=050603_Traveling_TheRoad_Together.html

"Saving Jews: Polish Righteous"
http://www.savingjews.org/righteous/zv.html

"Jozef Zwonarz" (wikipedia)
http://en.wikipedia.org/wiki/Jozef_Zwonarz

# Other titles from *Gihon River Press, Inc.*

## THE TATTERED PRAYER BOOK
By Ellen Bari and illustrated by Avi Katz

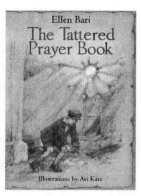

"What a sensitively written and beautifully illustrated book for parents, grandparents and educators to share with children! Ellen Bari's simple yet moving story coupled with exquisite line drawings by Avi Katz make The Tattered Prayer Book an age-appropriate resource for younger readers. No graphic violence is depicted. A nonthreatening yet accurate picture of the historical era is conveyed. The warmth and rich traditions of Jewish family life are experienced. In a world sadly still characterized by prejudice, hate, and discrimination, our students can instead be taught respect, tolerance, and a responsible, humane citizenship. With the power and desire to change life for the better, our children remain our hope for the future."

—**Dr. Margaret Lincoln, the District Librarian for Lakeview Schools in Battle Creek, Michigan, has served as a Teacher Fellow with the United States Holocaust Memorial Museum**
**ISBN: 978- 0-9819906-8-2     $18.95**

## URSULA'S PRISM
By Anna Block

"Ursula's Prism: The Holocaust through a Child's Eyes...A Survivor's Story", by Anna Block is based on a true story of survival, of a young girl against all odds trying to succeed in a world that couldn't care if she lives or dies. "Ursula's Prism" is a riveting work of fiction, highly recommended.
—**Midwest Book Review September 2011**
**Silver Medal Winner Presidents Book Award -**
**Florida Publishers Association 2011**
**ISBN: 978-0-9819906-2-0     $17.95**

## SILENCE NOT, A LOVE STORY
By Cynthia L. Cooper

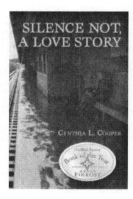

Cynthia Cooper is a powerful playwright. *Silence Not, A Love Story* will spark a fabulous discussion on resistance today. Gila and Paul have incredible moral courage and a life-long-love that sustains them through a terrible period in history when society failed. Each of us needs to consider our character at every moment—are we perpetrator, victim, helper, bystander, or resister? Every high school student should read this play.
—**Maureen McNeil, Director of Education,**
**The Anne Frank Center USA**
**ISBN: 978-0-9819906-0-6     $17.95**

### New for 2013 from *GIHON RIVER PRESS*

| May | August | December |
|---|---|---|
| AMIDST THE SHADOW OF TREES | THE STONES WEEP | WOMEN OF VALOR |
| by Miriam Brysk | by Margaret Lincoln and Miriam Brysk | by Joanne Gilbert |

Visit us on the web at www.gihonriverpress.com
To contact the publisher go to gihonriverpress@msn.com or call 917.612.8857